THE SECRETS OF FASHIONING

Ribbon Flowers

HEIRLOOMS FOR THE NEXT GENERATION

Helen Gibb

**krause
publications**

700 East State St., Iola, WI 54990-0001
Telephone 715-445-2214

Please call or write for our free catalog of
publications. Our toll-free number to place
an order or obtain a free catalog is
800-258-0929 or please use our regular
business telephone 715-445-2214 for
editorial comment and further information.

Designed by Jan Wojtech
Photography by Sara Frances, Important Occasions Photography, Denver, Colo.
Illustrations by Janice Page, Page Design, Buena Vista, Colo.
Manufactured in the United States of America

Kind thanks to the Art Institute of Chicago for permission to use "The Millinery Shop" by Edgar Degas.

Permission to use the Jane Austen quotes from the book *Jane Austen In Style*, by Susan Watkins, kindly
granted by Thames and Hudson, London, UK. Published 1996 © 1990 Susan Watkins.

Acknowledgment is made to Frederick Warne for permission to use the images on pages 78, 79, and 84.
Flower Fairies™ © Frederick Warne & Company 1997. Frederick Warne & Company is the owner of all
copyrights and trademarks of the Flower Fairies and illustrations. Licensed by Copyrights.

Library of Congress Cataloging-in-Publication Data

Gibb, Helen R.
    The secrets of fashioning ribbon flowers: heirlooms for the next generation

    p. 128

    ISBN 0-87341-562-0

1. Ribbon flowers   2. Crafts   3. Flowers

                                        97-74865

Dedication

This book is dedicated to Jim and Melinda, and to the many friends who have helped with the creative process.

Language of Flowers

Let me decipher you
the message of my
flow'rs:
The rose means
"love", the violet
"I am true".
Thus speak the lea-
ves that garland
fair Virginia's
bow'rs:
"In sunshine and
in grief I cling
to you".

C. Preston-Wynne.

A vintage postcard showing violets and roses. Dated 1910 on the back of the card.

Sincerest Greetings

Postcard dated 1911.

Credits

Loving thanks to my daughter, Melinda, for modeling the 1920's evening gown.

Bouquets to Kimberly Sode and Hanlie Wessels whose encouragement, helping hands, and enthusiasm were incredible. Gracious thanks to Vaban Gille, Inc. who provided me with many of the exquisite French and Swiss ribbons.

Thanks also go to Deb Legg of the White Hyacinth for making the beautiful pillows. Kudos to Barbara and the great team at Krause Publications for seeing the book through to fruition!

Without spectacular photos the book could have been very dull indeed and so I offer many thanks to my photographer, Sara Frances, for her beautiful imagery. Heartfelt thanks are also due to my friend and illustrator, Janice Page, who captured all the nuances of ribbon and interpreted my rough sketches by learning to make some of the ribbon flowers!

Thank you Tom Williams, curator of the Phipps Mansion in Denver, for the extensive use of that fabulous site for photography. Bouquets to Laurie Ramesbothom Watters at A Ladies Gallery for the use of her exquisite antiques seen in some of the photographs.

And a huge round of applause for the ladies who have tested my techniques. Thank you everyone!

TABLE of CONTENTS

Dedication 3
Credits 3
A Note from the Author 6

Chapter 1: An Introduction to Ribbon . . 8

Building a Ribbon Collection 10
Tools and Supplies 11

Chapter 2: Techniques 14

Fashioning Secrets and Other Tricks of the Trade. 15
Essential Ribbon Techniques. 15
Basic Techniques 16

Chapter 3: Fashioning the Flowers. . . 21

Pansies. 22
Violets 24
Sweet Peas 26
Poppies 28
Small Filler Flowers and Multi-Petal Blossoms . . 30
Canterbury Bells. 32
Bluebells 34
Berries and Rose Hips. 35
Hollyhocks. 36
Fuchsias. 38
Chrysanthemums 41
Delphiniums 42
Carnations 44
Peonies 45
Gardenias. 48
Leaves 50
Calyx. 54
Stems. 54

Chapter 4: Fashioning Roses 56

Gathered Roses 57
Folded Roses. 59
Wild Roses 61
Tea Roses 62
Cabochon Roses 66

Chapter 5: *Heirlooms for the Next Generation:*
The Ribbonwork Collection 68

Collage Brooch with Roses and Fuchsias 69
Ribbon Flowers in a Garden Urn 72
Framed Pansy Bouquet 74
Victorian Waxed Roses on a Box 76
Woodland Nest 78
Cabochon Rose Lampshade 80
Edwina in the Arbor 82
Topiary of Ivy and Roses 84
Miniature Rose Bouquet for a Crystal Vanity Box 86
Wildwood Brooch 88
Classic Rose Cushion 90
Victorian Purse Necklace 93
Wedding Rose Purse 96
Vintage Purse 98
Spring Hat with Fancy Peony 104
Vintage Summer Hat with Roses 106
Autumn Hat with Mixed Flowers 109
Winter Hat 112
Afternoon Tea and Tea Cozy 116
Beaded Fuchsias on a Cream Cushion 118

Glossary 120
About the Author 121
Bibliography 122
Resource Directory 123
Index. 126

A Note from the Author

Have you ever wondered how you became interested in a particular hobby, art, or craft? What was it that drew you? The subject matter, the colors, the medium, a project, a friend, a teacher, someone who said, "Come on. Try it! You can do it."

For me it was definitely the subject matter ~ flowers to be exact. Flowers have always been an inspiration for me. A favorite subject in my painting, these wonderful blooms showing off nature's fabulous colors have given me the freedom to create with much abandon.

It was while folding a ribbon that I realized the possibilities of flowers and ribbons. Together. Not just fresh flowers tied with ribbon, but flowers *made of* ribbon. Even though ribbons were a new medium for me, I was immediately intrigued by the challenge to create flowers that look just picked from the garden.

My interest in ribbons developed along with a growing fascination for fine period hats, particularly those from the late Victorian through the Edwardian era (roughly 1870 through 1910). Not only were some of these millinery confections full of ribbons, lace, flowers, leaves, and feathers, but sometimes they sported whole birds. Fabulous! My desire for more knowledge was insatiable.

I was able to study some ribbons and trims in detail when I purchased a traveling bonnet from the 1870s. However, it soon became apparent that more research was needed if I

was to pursue this new hat/ribbon/flower interest. I scoured antique shops, museums, libraries, and secondhand book shops, both in the United States and Australia. I also visited art galleries and was especially pleased to discover the Degas painting, *The Millinery Shop,* in The Art Institute of Chicago, along with several other paintings depicting ladies and hats! All of this research, of course, helped add to my book and hat collections.

A selection of hats from Edward Ridley & Sons millinery catalog, circa 1880.

One great source for ribbon and hat information has been millinery books and women's magazine articles from the turn of the century through the 1920s. These explain all the details of bow and flower making as well as how to trim and construct hats. Other valuable sources of information are reprints of catalogs from Montgomery Ward and Co., Sears, The National Cloak and Suit Co., and others dating from late Victorian and Edwardian times. Several catalogs have ribbon and millinery sections describing the hats available for sale and include such wonderful information as ribbon color, flower type, and price.

My research also involved interviewing family and friends. When I asked them specifically about certain ribbon trims, they shared memories of special dresses:

"When I was six years old I had a white embroidered dress with a four-inch ribbon sash and a

Edgar Degas, French, 1834-1917, The Millinery Shop, oil on canvas; 1884/90, 100 x 110.7 cm, Mr. and Mrs. Lewis Larned Coburn Memorial Collection, 1933.428. Photograph © 1997, The Art Institute of Chicago. All Rights Reserved.

bow in pink. Or was it blue? There was a matching hat of ribbon straw with the same color ribbon trim.

I was quite a bit older when I wore a bridesmaid dress of royal blue velvet with a slightly lighter tone of royal blue ruched ribbon roses on it. Also a hat with the same roses, wound around until it reached about four inches across. I didn't have a dress with cabochon roses on it, but I saw several with the roses at the waist."

Idrys Perry Buesnel, Jersey, Channel Islands, January 1997, age 82

"Oh dear, it's been so long ago. I don't remember cabochon roses, but I do remember lovely green and white ribbon rosettes on one of my dresses when I was a young girl."

Leigh Deering, Adelaide, Australia, December 1996, age 82

"I have a few treasures from my mother and grandmother. Let's see now ~ a black velvet cape with embroidered jet trim, a fur muff, a bonnet . . . This photo is my mother giving her high school graduation speech in 1894. The dress was a pale gold with a lot of ribbon trim around the neckline. And look at all those pleats. They really knew how to make beautiful dresses in those days."

*Emily Gibb, Illinois,
July 1997, age 79*

This pleated, pale gold silk dress is trimmed with ribbons around the neckline. Anita Pence Purdum, high school graduation speech, 1894. (Photo courtesy of Emily Gibb)

Have you asked your relatives and friends what they remember? Perhaps they might tell or show you something truly wonderful.

I had the good fortune to acquire a fabulous piece of ribbonwork ~ a 1920's evening gown decorated with delicate cabochon roses.

The dress fabric is autumn gold silk georgette with a spray of ribbon cabochon roses resting on an overlay of gold metallic lace at the shoulder. The bows in the back are eight-inch-wide silk with the same bright pink ribbon roses and forget-me-nots nestled into the folds wending their way up the back of the dress.

There is also a capelet (jacket) made of the same dress fabric and trimmed with fur, a truly beautiful period piece. The dress was originally made in the 1920s for Mrs. Endlich who owned an exclusive dress shop in Topeka, Kansas. Alas, I have no other history about this dress.

Armed with classic ribbon techniques, I set out to

make many of the flowers described in the old millinery books but soon found myself creating new flowers and new techniques. So enamored had I become with ribbonwork that I realized the need to share these flower techniques with others. And so, here you hold the result of my ribbon passion.

Detail from circa 1925 dress. The main cabochon rose has eight large petals and the smaller rose has three petals.

This book re-creates for you the old ribbon techniques and transforms old flower favorites into blooms that are still popular today ~ roses, pansies, hollyhocks, gardenias, sweet peas, and many more. It is not my intention to give you a project book, but to create a book of flower techniques with classic applications for your new ribbon flowers. It is also my hope that you will be inspired and encouraged enough by this new knowledge to expand and fulfill your own creative instincts. Come on, try it! You can do it!

Ribbonwork is beautiful, and as such should be passed on to the next generation. Perhaps the flowers you make and put on a hat or dress today will one day inspire someone from another era to become interested in ribbonwork.

Helen Gibb

Chapter 1:
An Introduction to Ribbon

"... *my gown is to be trimmed everywhere with white ribbon plaited somehow or other.*"
Jane Austen, 1813

Vintage dress with ribbon rose decoration, circa 1925.

Many reliable books have been written about the history of clothing which happily include the role of ribbon as a decoration on dresses, hats, and bonnets. The Jane Austen quote is from the book *Jane Austen, In Style* by Susan Watkins who describes the lifestyle of Austen, her family, and her home through the letters she wrote. There are many references to dresses, hats, and other ladies accessories loaded with ribbon trimmings which were very popular at that time. When I read this book, I was immediately drawn into the life of the early 1800s. It's unbelievable how much energy and effort was put into dress and bonnet decisions. Just imagine all those stitches!

This same energy is evident when perusing the pages of the *Ladies Home Journal* and other Victorian and Edwardian magazines and clothing catalogs. The information on style ~ whether it is in dress or home ~ and the sections on millinery and needlework are all extremely informative and entertaining, creating a window to the past. Not only do we learn how to crochet doilies, make a hat, a flower, or a milliner's bow, but we can read the descriptions for cleaning lace and other household hints.

Millinery and cloak catalog, 1898.

Some turn-of-the-century mail order catalogs also have pages of ribbons for sale, with full descriptions of ribbon type, color, and price. Imagine a two-inch-wide taffeta ribbon selling for 12 cents a yard! In one 1908 catalog, the following offer was made for purchases over one dollar: ". . . we make this most liberal free offer of a special publication . . . written for us by an expert. This valuable book is an education on how to make bows for the hair and millinery purposes, and also instructions on how to make a great many fancy articles such as ribbon girdles, glove boxes, opera bags and floral effects."

A transition in the role of ribbon is evident during the 1920s. Here we see the beautiful use of ribbons as smaller and simpler decorations on clothing and in millinery. A strong emphasis, however, continued with the popular "craft" use of ribbon in items such as powder puffs, hand mirrors, pin cushions, sashes, slippers, and other items in a lady's boudoir.

Today you may still come upon samples of ribbonwork from the 1920s. Should you be so fortunate, please handle these treasures gently. By all means study the craftsmanship closely and feel inspired to try to re-create what you see. But remember, old ribbons can be very fragile.

If you have some old ribbon, I recommend that you keep it intact and enjoy its beauty as it is. You wouldn't want to use the very old ribbons in your new work since they are already stressed by age. However, ribbon from the 1950s is still available and can be safely used with care.

The time has come to revive ribbonwork and bring it into the 1990s. Because we don't wear large fancily trimmed hats or heavily decorated dresses, our creative energies can be directed to adapting these designs for simpler clothing decoration, beautiful accessories for our homes, and as gifts to give our families and friends.

Re-create a vintage hat using the old ribbon techniques and make it a decorative piece for a bedroom or hall tree. Cover a plain paper hatbox with wallpaper and decorate the top with yards of ribbon, lace, and flowers. Make up dozens of mixed flowers and arrange them in a vase or wrap them in lace or tulle for a lavish table display. Gift boxes can be wrapped, then trimmed in ribbon flowers. Little girls will love a hair bow decorated with tiny multi-petal flowers to match the same flowers on her shoes! And wouldn't you love to wear a fabulous ribbon purse necklace or carry a vintage-inspired purse to your next special occasion? Try ribbon corsages for the next wedding you plan. . .
Shall we start?

Building a Ribbon Collection

ribbon is a French one known as *lignes*, with the sizes designated numerically, e.g. #3 (5/8″/15mm), #5 (7/8″/23mm), #9 (1½″/39mm), and so on. This is the system manufacturers use to sell ribbon to wholesalers and retailers. Consumers purchase ribbon according to its width in inches (or the metric equivalent).

I used a variety of ribbon sizes for the ribbonwork in this book. To simplify the instructions, I have rounded up some of the widths (3/4″ for #3, 1″ for #5, 1½″ for #9). When buying ribbons, select a range of widths, with most of your choices being 1″ and 1½″.

Ribbon Quality: French wired ribbons can be made of polyester or rayon acetate. Experiment with both types. After a while you may develop a preference for one over the other. My preference is rayon acetate. Avoid craft quality and cut edge ribbons because they are too stiff. A soft supple touch to the ribbon is essential for successful ribbonwork.

Color and Texture: Remember, variation in the palette is the secret to making stunning flowers. Don't be afraid of that yellow/orange ombre ~ it makes a great pansy petal, hollyhock center, or a superb rose. Try a half yard of the citrus green ~ it's fabulous for a poppy center and calyx or an eye-popping accent leaf.

When adapting a flower for fashion or home decor, texture plays just as important a role as color so don't overlook ribbons such as velvet, silk, organdy, and wired grosgrain. Look at a striped or embossed ribbon as an accent petal or leaf. Try some organdy ribbon to create a freeform folded rose. Treat yourself to a quarter yard of expensive woven jacquard for a purse necklace. My ribbon buying motto is: If you like it, buy it! And if you're not sure if you like it, buy a small piece anyway! You'll find a use for it sometime.

Here are my suggestions for flower colors: three yards each of pale pink, mauve, plum, and peach; one yard each of purple and lavender; two yards each of at

As you become more involved in ribbon art, your tastes will become defined and you will have a better idea of what types and colors of ribbons you prefer. My suggestions are merely that ~ suggestions to help you get started.

Types: Most of the flowers and projects in this book are made from French wired ribbons in a variety of widths and colors. Because some flower techniques are not suitable for woven ribbons, I have also used bias cut silk ribbons. Within these two groups you will find a huge palette of colors, ranging from solids to ombres to crossweaves to hand-dyed ribbons. The silk ribbons give a wonderfully soft touch to the flower petals, while the wired ribbons allow you to style the petals once the flower is complete.

Sizes: The system for measuring the width of wired

least three shades of green (blue/green, olive ombre, forest); one yard each of pale yellow, yellow/orange ombre, autumn gold, rust; three yards of cream; two yards of off-white; and a yard of any other color that you absolutely must have! I have even bought ribbon to use later without having something specific in mind and it's come in very handy when it's midnight and the great idea strikes!

Note: Before you begin the ribbonwork pieces in this book, please be aware that exact ribbon widths and lengths are only given for each *petal*, so you may have to add up the inches to get the exact yardage required. It is assumed that you will have enough ribbon on hand to at least practice a flower or two. If I quote a yardage amount, it will be enough to complete the piece, with possibly some left over. Be sure to read *all* the instructions before cutting any ribbon.

Ribbon Storage: What to do? Here's an idea. Roll your ribbons around a tube or your fingers, being care- ful not to crease the wires. Put the rolled ribbon into an acid free cardboard box, plastic drawer, or lined basket. If you buy ribbon by the roll, simply keep the rolls stored in large plastic trays with lids. Stack the trays under a work table when not needed.

Cleaning Ribbon: Most ribbon ~ used flat or slightly ruffled and stitched securely to a dress ~ should stand up to a gentle wash in warm water. Some ribbons are not colorfast, so do a test if you're unsure.

I am very cautious about washing ribbon after it is made up into a dimensional flower and applied to clothing. It is much safer to make the piece removable. Use a brooch pin or stitch the flowers to crinoline which in turn can be removed for cleaning. The 1920's dress on page 8 has rose sprays attached to crinoline which is only lightly stitched to the dress. Most of the applications for ribbons in this book would not require washing.

Tools and Supplies

Needles: I prefer size 9 and 10 milliner's needles. They are similar to a sharp except they are long and thin and quite adaptable as a beading needle if necessary. These long needles make quick work of gathering and stitching through thick layers of ribbon.

Thread: Use size #33 beading thread in either black or white. It's thin yet strong, and will withstand the rigorous tightening of gathering stitches that ribbonwork sometimes demands. Since most stitches won't be visible, use white thread with light colored ribbon and black thread with dark ribbon. Don't worry, everything will blend into the shadows.

A good thread length is 15 inches ~ long enough to get the job done but not too long to get knotted or tangled. Single thread is sufficient. Buttonhole twist or quilting thread is also usable but can be too heavy for some of the very fine ribbons.

FASHIONING SECRET

If you have the misfortune to have a white stitch show, simply color it with a fine point artist's felt tip marker in a color to blend with the ribbon (be careful not to stain the ribbon). The alternative is to leave it alone or re-stitch.

Scissors: Whatever you do, don't use your best dressmaking scissors on wired ribbon! The blades will become dull. Buy a pair of inexpensive sharp scissors with at least a four-inch blade that will cut the ribbon cleanly. Have a pair of fine point embroidery scissors on hand for trimming thread and getting into those tiny places that are too small for the ribbon scissors.

Crinoline: This is an old-fashioned material used in dress and hat making. It looks and feels like stiffened netting or cheesecloth. Some ribbonwork requires stitching the flowers and leaves to a crinoline base before securing it to a blouse, pillow, or purse. This allows you to remove the ribbonwork should you need to clean the base item. Collage brooches are also created by stitching all the elements to crinoline.

You can buy crinoline by the yard at some fabric shops or from some of the vendors in the resource section of this book. A half yard of black and a half yard of white will see you through many projects.

Stamens: These little beauties make any flower come to life! They are mostly double-headed and are sold in bunches of about 100. They're not always easy to find, so it's worth buying as many stamen styles and colors as you can, but avoid buying plastic ones.

For realism don't be afraid to mix colors, particularly on roses. If you don't have any stamens and are really desperate for them, you can raid your best silk flower and rip it apart for the stamens (I did this on two of the roses in the large floral arrangement). For an elegant look, try some jeweled or pearl varieties.

Long Pins: Let's face it, we're not all nimble fingered. In fact, most of you will feel all thumbs when you first begin working with ribbons, but don't despair, this feeling will disappear with experience and time.

Purchase some long thin sharp pins to hold things in place until you are ready to stitch permanently. These are invaluable in making composite designs where you have many elements to contend with. Trimming hats and making collage brooches definitely requires some extra fingers. A word of caution ~ pins may leave a hole in the ribbon so be sure to pin in an inconspicuous place such as a fold or valley in the ribbon.

Ruler/Tape Measure: Buy one that shows both inches and centimeters.

Tailor's Awl: This handy sharply pointed tool is ideal for poking holes in fabric. It's also great for wrapping thin wire to make "curly cues" or tendrils for the sweet peas.

Stem Wire: Use cloth-covered wire for the stems of your flowers. It comes in a variety of gauges with the most useful being 18- or 20-gauge for big flower stems, 22-gauge for medium flowers, and 30- or 32-gauge for small flowers and florets that are later attached to a main flower stem. Most wire is sold in 18-inch lengths.

Needle Nose Pliers with Wire Cutter: You'll need these for cutting stem wire and forming tiny loops in the wire.

Floral Tape: Most floral supply shops carry three or four colors of paper floral tape. I recommend you buy two colors of green. Use it to cover the raw edges of flowers and to cover the wire stem. Store floral tape in plastic baggies when not in use.

Thread Wrap: Use embroidery floss, perle cotton #5, or silk embroidery thread as an alternative to floral tape to wrap the base of a flower and stem so that all the messy ends and wires are neatly covered.

Cotton Wadding/Batting: You'll use this for stuffing buds, berries, and rose hips. Choose cotton rather than polyester fiberfill because it compacts better. Cotton balls are a good substitute.

Tube or Loop Turner: Sold in quilt and fabric shops, this handy tool helps turn tubes of bias silk ribbon inside out. (For an example, study the stem tubes on the Framed Pansy Bouquet on page 74.)

Collect millinery trims such as these dear little pink velvet flowers and use them as filler flowers in your ribbonwork.

Beads, Buttons, Lace, and Other Essential Bits and Pieces: Needless to say, some ribbon projects require embellishing, so I encourage you to stock up on a variety of beads, buttons, and small pieces of old lace. Vintage millinery supplies are also worth collecting and using in ribbonwork. Keep on hand some silk veiling, mini flowers, leaves, feathers, stamens, and hatpins.

Chapter 2:
Techniques

Fashioning Secrets and Other Tricks of the Trade

❀ When ribbon is cut, it can become frayed after a little use. To avoid "hairy" edges, dab a little Fray Check™ on the freshly cut edge of the ribbon.

❀ Fabric glue or tacky glue works well for wrapping thread or ribbon around the stems of flowers, but use it lightly and sparingly and always test a scrap of ribbon before applying.

❀ If you absolutely detest stitching, you may use a hot glue gun and glue stick to assemble the flowers after all the petals have been stitched. However, I *don't* recommend glue for any wearable or soft furnishing piece. (Mass production work for resale would be an exception.)

❀ Steaming a ribbon flower that has become a little squashed or rumpled will give it new life. I have done this to several of my antique hats when the bows have softly fallen over and to the roses on the 1920's dress with great success. Simply place the article to be revived over a steaming tea kettle or pot of boiling water until the ribbon is pliable. Reshape the ribbon and remove it from the steam. A commercial steamer is also an option. To assist you in the shaping process and so your fingers aren't hurt by the hot steam, use a smooth-edged tool, a cotton swab, or pad the ends of a pair of tweezers with something soft.

❀ Sometimes a stitch pattern requires you to remove one wire from the ribbon for easier gathering or stitching. To remove a wire, simply expose it at the cut edge of the ribbon and pull it out as shown below.

❀ A note to left-handed stitchers: Please feel free to stitch and fold ribbons from whichever direction you are most comfortable with.

Essential Ribbon Techniques

"I have determined to trim my lilac sarsenet with black sattin ribbon... Ribbon trimmings are all the fashion at Bath."　Jane Austen, 1814

Postcard manufactured around 1915 depicting an artist's impression of 19th century ladies.

Ribbon techniques are well described in the magazines and millinery books dating from the turn of the century through the 1920s. From these I learned most of the ribbon basics that follow. Please take time to read this section, as it is the basis for all the flowers in the book.

STITCHES

1. A **backstitch** is one stitch on top of another when securing thread. Begin and end all stitching by securing the thread with three or four backstitches. If you knot the thread, be sure to secure it with one or two backstitches before you begin stitching. If you don't knot the thread, start the stitching with three or four backstitches. Ribbonwork often requires a lot of tight gathering and if the thread is not secured well, it will pull out when you begin to gather the ribbon.

2. **Running stitches** or **gathering stitches** are quickly-made straight stitches used to gather ribbon. Most of the stitches are hidden in the folds of the ribbon so don't worry too much about "pretty stitching." Ribbonwork is to be enjoyed, so you have permission to be a wee bit uneven in your gathering stitches!

3. The **stitch length** can be anywhere from 1/16″ to 1/2″ or longer, depending on the width and length of the ribbon used. With the ribbon widths I used, most of the stitch lengths are about 1/16″ to 1/4″. There is a fine balance here and only experimentation will determine what looks and feels right.

4. Use the **stab stitch** to stitch ribbons, flowers, and leaves to hats and collage brooches. Push the needle down through the ribbon and pull it through to the other side (similar to the beginning of a cross stitch).

5. **French knots** were often used in vintage ribbonwork to enhance the main flower. Typically, an embroidery thread was used to make the forget-me-not flowers but you can successfully substitute silk embroidery ribbon for a slightly fuller flower. To make a French knot, refer to your favorite stitchery book or use the method shown below.

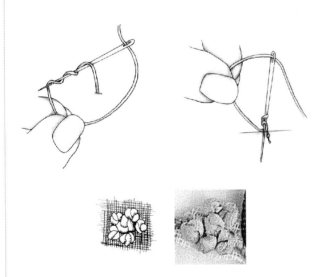

Basic Techniques

With only a handful of techniques you can fashion a variety of flowers in a multitude of colors. These techniques can be used singly or in combination. Some flowers are made from a single length of ribbon while others are fashioned from several pieces of ribbon.

The techniques are **folding, rolling, gathering, petals, knots, tubes,** and **stems.** Familiarize yourself with each technique by studying the illustrations and learning the stitch patterns. Make several practice petals and affix the best of them to a piece of cardboard for reference when you make a flower using that technique.

FOLDING

Folding and twisting the ribbon is often the fastest way to make a flower.

The folded rose shown is a good example of ribbon simply folded and stitched in place. Detailed instructions for this rose are on page 59.

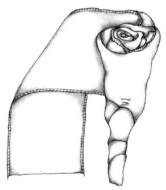

ROLLING

Roll up or coil any length of ribbon, gathered or flat, to form a flower (see the gathered rose, carnation, and chrysanthemum).

When rolling ribbon it is important that the top edges of the flower are level and even, as well as the bottom edge.

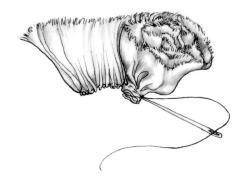

GATHERING

Sometimes you will gather ribbon on a wire and other times you will use running stitches to gather the ribbon. Depending on the flower you're making, the gathering may be tight or loose.

Gathering Ribbon on the Wire is simple, but be careful not to pull out the wire or ruin the edging that encloses the wire. Expose the wires ~ about 1/2″ at one end of a piece of ribbon ~ and twist them together securely.

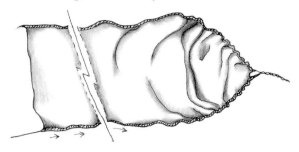

From the opposite end, gently draw the ribbon along one wire until the length of ribbon is gathered. To secure the gathering, simply twist the ending wires together. Use this technique to make ruffles and gathered roses.

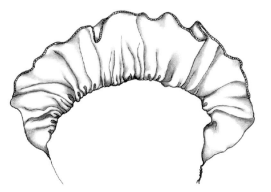

Straight Gathering—Use straight gathering only on bias silk ribbon because its cut edges don't unravel like woven, wired ribbon. Stitch across the length of the ribbon about 1/8″ from the edge, gather to the desired fullness, and secure. I used this technique when making the carnations and peony centers.

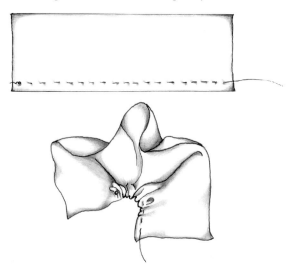

U-Gathering—Named for its "u" shape stitch pattern, this is the most versatile gathering stitch pattern for petals. U-gathers can be single petals (flat and rolled edged) or up to five continuous petals. All ribbon widths are suitable for this technique with the length adjusted proportionally. *Remember:* Always remove the wire from the gathering side of the ribbon when stitching a u-gather petal.

For a single petal, practice with a 1½″ wide x 4″ long piece of ribbon. Stitch along the edges as shown, leaving 1/8″ allowance at each short end.

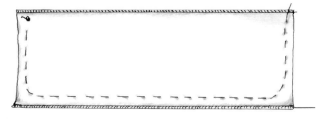

Gather and secure the thread. The shape of the petal is determined by the length of the ribbon.

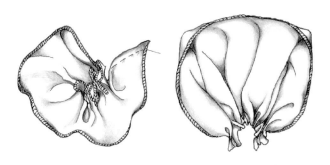

Single u-gathered petals are used on the poppies, sweet peas, hollyhock leaves, some gathered roses, and small fantasy flowers.

Rolled Edge U-Gathering—The rolled edge version of the single u-gather is used for the cabochon rose petals and is made by tightly rolling down 1/3 of the ribbon width on one edge, then stitching the u-shape pattern.

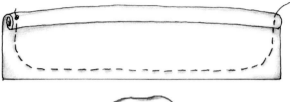

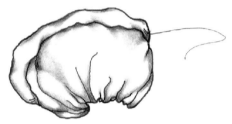

Continuous U-Gathering—A series of u-gathers stitched along one length of ribbon will result in multiple petals strung together ready to attach to stamen centers. I call this a continuous u-gather stitch pattern. To achieve the best petal shape and ease in gathering, note the stitch pattern showing how the thread hooks over the top edges of the ribbon.

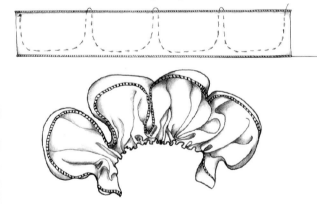

The pansy and violet use two and three continuous u-gathers for their petals. Four or five continuous u-gathers give you a variety of blossoms (apple, cherry, geranium, hydrangea), a filler flower, or a beautiful rose center.

PETALS

For a change of pace in your ribbon techniques, try these two old petal techniques ~ dipped corners and rolled corners. They are very striking because of their life-like appearance. Use ribbons that are 1″ or wider. For both styles of petals, practice with wired ribbon 1½″ wide x 3″ long.

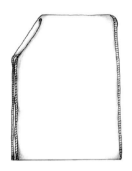

Dipped Corner

1. Remove both wires and fold over the ribbon as shown.

2. Tuck in the corners and stitch the edge about 1/2″ down from the fold to secure the tucks. Cut the thread.

FASHIONING SECRET
For the dipped and rolled corner petals, try to hide your stitches by stitching from the inside of the folded ribbon.

3. Make pleats at the bottom of the ribbon, with both left and right pleats folded toward the center. Secure the pleats with backstitches.

I used this technique on the waxed wild roses, some of the blended tea roses, and the inner petals of the gardenia.

Rolled Corner

This is *the* rose petal technique everyone wants to learn so they can make gorgeous roses. The finished petal looks like a mature rose petal with its edges starting to curl under. To achieve this look, it takes a little patience and practice before you feel confident.

"The petals of the fetching little rose may be made from one-and-one-fourth inch ribbon. For one like the model shown, six pieces, a little more than two inches in length, will be required." Photograph and text from Needlecraft, April 1915.

1. Fold a 1½″ wide x 3″ long piece of ribbon in half. Do not remove the wires. With the folded side at the top, fold over 1/4″ of ribbon at the left corner.

2. Roll this again at the same angle. *Note:* For different petal shapes change the angle and the depth of each roll.

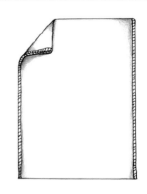

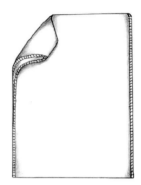

3. Secure this roll with 2-3 tiny hidden backstitches. I find it easiest to make the hidden stitches from inside the folded ribbon. The goal is to have no stitches showing on the rolled edge of the petal. Do not cut the thread.

4. Fold the right corner of the folded ribbon just like you did with the left corner. Using the thread carried across from the first rolled corner, stitch the right roll from the inside. Again, aim for hidden stitches. Cut the thread.

5. Turn the ribbon petal around so the rolled corners are in the back. With the front of the petal facing you, make two pleats in the same direction at the bottom edge. The pleats will make the petal cup shaped. Stitch

across the bottom about 1/4″ from the edge, being sure to catch all the pleats. Cut the thread.

6. When making a rose, these petals are stitched with the rolled corners facing away from the center of the rose. This petal is used on all the tea roses.

KNOTS

Small pieces of ribbon knotted at the middle can be used as flower centers, miniature buds, or as petals. I used knots for the chrysanthemum petals and the hollyhock centers.

TUBES

The tube technique is useful as a petal substitute for hollyhocks, Canterbury bells, bluebells, berries, and calyx.

1. Fold a length of ribbon with right sides together and stitch a tiny seam along the raw edges. Secure the thread.
2. Finger press the seam over to one side. Refer to the instructions for the particular flower, berry or calyx to finish the piece.

Long tubes of bias cut silk ribbon make wonderful stem covers for flowers in a posy. Fold the ribbon lengthwise and stitch down the long side. Turn right side out with a loop turner. The pansy bouquet uses these stem tubes.

STEMS

Stem wire can be attached to the flower by several methods. One way is to poke a hole in the base of the flower, cover the tip of the wire with glue, and insert it into the hole. Another way is to bend a tiny loop at the top of the wire and glue or stitch inside the first flower petal before constructing the rest of the flower.

Another method is to wrap thin wire around the center of the stamens, then stitch or glue the wire to the first petal.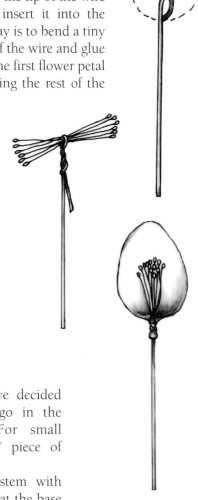

If stemming flowers for a large floral arrangement, use an 18″ length of wire and trim it after you have decided where it will go in the arrangement. For small flowers, a 2″-4″ piece of wire will suffice.

To wrap a stem with floral tape, start at the base of the flower, covering all the raw edges of the ribbon and any stray stitches. Angle the wrap and start rolling the tape between your thumb and first finger at an angle around and down the wire until it's covered. If you stretch the tape a bit as you go, it will stick to itself better.

For a dressier treatment of the stems, you can use embroidery floss, perle cotton #5, or silk embroidery thread to wrap the base of a flower and stem to cover the raw edges and wire. A touch of fabric glue over the base of the flower is all you need to get the wrapping started. A few more dabs of glue along the wire will hold the rest of the wrapping in place. The leaf stems on the gardenias, pink peony, waxed flower posy, and the cabochon rose spray are all thread wrapped.

Chapter 3:
Fashioning the Flowers

A rhapsody of ribbon flowers ~ roses, poppies, carnations, delphiniums, and sweet peas.

Pansies

ecause they bloom in the early spring and summer, these sweet little flowers with smiling faces and bright colors are nature's welcoming committee in the garden. Stroll along a path of pansies and note the array of colors so you will know what color combinations to use on your ribbon pansy. Keep in mind the more unusual colors ~ soft peach, rust, burgundy, and pale lavender ~ in addition to the traditional purples and yellows.

In the Victorian language of flowers, pansies mean thoughtfulness. Wrap the pansies in a small doily, tie a ribbon around the stems, and present them to someone special. Pansies also look sweet in a tiny crystal vase mixed with a few u-gather blossoms. They stand alone as lovely flower brooches or can be arranged in a group and framed. Ombre ribbons work very well for pansies because of the two-toned effect. Before you cut the ribbon, decide which edge color will be the outside edge of the flower petals. For a realistically sized pansy, use 1″-wide ribbons.

Boat leaves (page 51) 1″ wide x 5″ long, folded in half widthwise, are suitable for pansy leaves.

1. Each pansy is made using the continuous u-gather technique in two phases, making the back two petals first and then the three front petals. For the back petals, cut a 6¼″ long piece of 1″-wide ribbon.

2. Remove the wire from the gathering edge and crease the ribbon at the halfway point (3⅛″).

The chameleon-like quality of ombre ribbons is perfect for the new pansies shown on this antique crocheted purse.

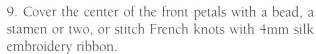

3. Stitch two continuous u-gathers (one in each section), leaving 1/8″ margins at each raw edge. Tightly gather the ribbon as you go and secure it when all is gathered.

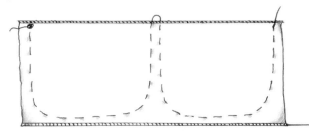

4. Attach these petals to a 1″ circle of crinoline, near the gathered edge. Set aside.

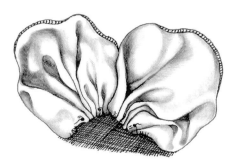

5. For the three front petals, cut a 10¼″ long piece of 1″-wide ribbon.

6. Remove the wire from the gathering edge. Fold the ribbon into three sections, measuring from left to right, 3⅛″, 4″, and 3⅛″.

7. Stitch three continuous u-gathers, again leaving 1/8″ margins at each raw edge.

8. Tightly gather the ribbon after each section, finish gathering, and secure. Join the ends by stitching the beginning stitch to the last stitch. The center should be quite tight. If not, weave your thread back and forth across the middle, catching the ribbon in the folds near the center's edge and tighten.

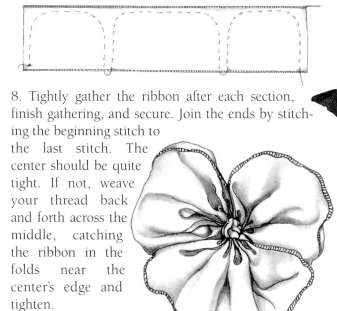

9. Cover the center of the front petals with a bead, a stamen or two, or stitch French knots with 4mm silk embroidery ribbon.

10. Place the front petals on top of and slightly below the two back petals on the crinoline so the back petals peek out. Stitch in place.

11. Trim the excess crinoline and cover the back of the pansy with a piece of ribbon.

Stems

12. If you are stemming the pansy, make a loop in a piece of 32-gauge wire and stitch or glue it to the back of the crinoline before covering it with ribbon.

13. Fold in the raw edges of the covering ribbon, pierce a hole in the center, and slip it over the stem. Glue or stitch it to the back of the pansy.

14. Wrap the stems with floral tape, bias cut ribbon, or perle cotton or make stem tubes from bias cut ribbon for a soft bouquet look.

Violets

Whether wild in the woods or in a carefully tended garden, these tiny spring blossoms are sweet when cut and displayed in small vases. For ribbon violets, old perfume bottles make pretty containers (Mum's idea). Scatter violets across a hat, make a posy, or tuck them behind another flower in a collage brooch. These are very versatile filler flowers!

Some of the violet techniques described in the old books used knotted narrow ribbons but I prefer a fuller flower and so have designed a violet using the **u-gather technique.** Use 1/2″- or 3/4″-wide wired or unwired ribbons in a selection of lavenders and purples. Silk embroidery ribbons, 13mm wide, and 5/8″-wide bias cut silk ribbons also work well for violets.

The centers can be French knots of 4mm yellow silk embroidery ribbon, yellow stamens, yellow seed beads, or one larger bead. Prairie point or boat leaves (page 51) work well for violet leaves.

Recycle an old perfume bottle and fill it with ribbon violets.

1. Violets are made in two steps using the **continuous u-gather** technique with two separate pieces of ribbon. The construction method is similar to the pansy. Try to mix and match colors for variety. Cut a 3¼″ length of ribbon for the back two petals and a 4¾″ length for the three front petals. These measurements include 1/8″ margins on each side of the cut edge. If the ribbon is wired, remove the wire on the gathering edge.

2. Fold the shorter piece in half and crease the ribbon to mark the center. Stitch a u-shape in each half, gathering the ribbon tightly as you go. Secure the thread and cut.

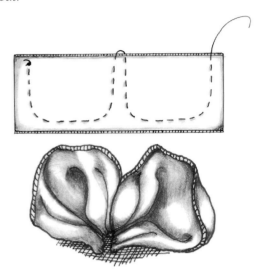

3. Fold the longer piece in thirds and crease the fabric to mark each third. Stitch a continuous u-gather in each third, gathering tightly as you go. Secure the thread and join the ends together, being sure the center is tight. Secure and cut the thread. Cover the center with a French knot of 4mm yellow silk embroidery ribbon, stamens, or seed beads.

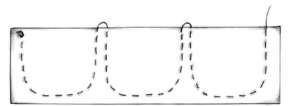

4. Stitch the back petals to a 1″ piece of crinoline. Place the front three petals on top of and slightly below the back petals. Stitch in place and trim the excess crinoline.

Stems

5. If you are stemming the violet, make a loop in a piece of 32-gauge wire and stitch or glue it to the back of the crinoline before covering it with ribbon.

6. Fold in the raw edges of the covering ribbon, pierce a hole in the center, and slip it over the stem. Glue or stitch it to the back of the violet.

7. Wrap the stem with floral tape, bias cut ribbon, or perle cotton.

Sweet Peas

According to the language of flow-ers, sweet pea means "delicate pleasure," which is quite appropriate if compared to a sweet baby in a bonnet! Use these blossoms in arrangements of mixed flowers, in posies, or on hats.

A realistic stem of sweet peas is made by using two different ribbon widths, two different colors of ribbon, and four or five florets on one stem. Choose solids and ombres in salmon, pink, cream, and lavender.

Sweet peas are most realistic if you use two ribbon widths and two coordinating ribbons. Ombre ribbons are an excellent choice.

1. The three parts of the sweet pea are made with the **single u-gather technique.** The outer petal is a 6″ length of 1½″-wide ribbon; the middle petal is a 5″ length of 1″-wide ribbon; and the center pea is a 1½″ length of 1″-wide ribbon. Remove the wire on the gathering side of the ribbon.

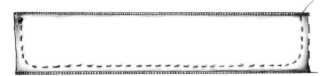

2. Stitch the center pea and stitch or hot glue a 3″ piece of 32-gauge wire (with a small loop at the end) to the inside of the pea.

3. Gather tightly (the pea will be cupped). Secure the thread, then flatten the pea as shown. Bend the wired side of the pea backwards.

4. Stitch and gather the middle petal so it fits around the base of the center pea. Secure it to the pea.

5. Gather the outer petal so it will fit around the base of both the small petal and pea. (This reminds me of a baby with a double-frilled sun bonnet on its head.)

6. Make four more stemmed florets as described above.

7. Use floral tape to cover any raw edges at the base of the florets and wires.

Bud & Tendrils

8. Make the bud for the top of the stem by stitching and styling a 2½″ length of 1½″-wide ribbon in the same manner as the center pea. Glue it to an 18″ length of 20-gauge wire and style by scrunching it tight.

9. Make some tendrils (the little curly-cues that hold the sweet pea on the trellis) by curling 2″-3″ pieces of 32-gauge wire around a loop turner, knitting needle, crochet hook, or other similar object.

Stems

10. Begin the stemming process with the bud. Use floral tape to cover the raw edges of the bud ribbon and 1″ of the main stem. Add the florets and tendrils to the main stem as shown.

FASHIONING SECRET

The secret to pretty sweet peas is in the styling of the petals. The back petal should flare out, while the top of the middle petal should be pinched to a point.

Poppies

With their crepe paper-like petals and vibrant crisp colors, who could resist these fabulous flowers? Of all the poppy varieties available, my ribbon version most closely resembles the Iceland poppy found in many gardens in the spring.

Try orange, peach, yellow, cream, and sherbet pink colors, all of which have appeared in my garden. Use solid or ombre colors. I chose 1″-wide citrus or lime green for the poppy centers, the calyx, and bud cup even though real poppies have a tiny bit of yellow at the base of each petal and a yellow center. The 25 double-headed yellow stamens around the green center really set this flower off to perfection.

You will also need some green floral tape, 20-gauge stem wire, and a small amount of cotton wadding.

Show off your ribbon poppies in brightly colored glass bottles.

1. The poppy petals are made with the **single u-gather technique.** The poppy has four petals, all cut from 1½″-wide ribbon. Cut two 6″ lengths and two 7″ lengths.

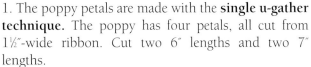

2. Make the center of the flower by covering the top of a stem wire with a pea-sized piece of cotton wadding. Cover that with a 1″ square of green ribbon with both wires removed and secure with thread.

3. Fold the stamens in half and position them around this center. Tightly wrap thread around them,

then secure them in place with a few stitches. The top of the stamens should come about halfway up on the poppy petal.

4. Remove the wire on the gathering edge of the ribbon and make four single u-gathered petals from the 6″ and 7″ lengths. Gather the 6″ petals more tightly than the 7″ petals.

5. Stitch one of the 6″ petals, snugly fitting, around the base of the stamen center. Stitch the other 6″ petal opposite the first.

6. Stitch one of the 7″ petals between and on the outside of the first two petals. Stitch the other 7″ petal opposite that. Keep the top of the petals level with the previous row of petals. Refer to the diagram below for petal placement.

7. Hide the raw edges at the bottom of the flower with a green tube calyx 1″ wide x 2¾″ long. Be sure the tube is right side out.

   Slipstitch the tube to the underside of the poppy, then wrap thread around the ribbon and stem. Secure the thread and wrap the stem with floral tape.

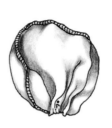

Bud

8. Cut one 4″ length for the bud petal. Make a u-gather petal. Scrunch it up and glue the petal to a piece of 20-gauge stem wire.

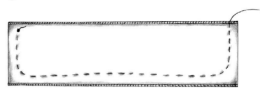

9. Make a u-gather bud cup from citrus green ribbon (1″ wide x 2½″ long). Gather and stitch it to the petal. It will cover half the bud petal. Cover the raw edges and the stem with floral tape.

FASHIONING SECRET
Crimp the edges of the poppy petals like you would crimp a pie crust.

Small Filler Flowers and Multi-Petal Blossoms

As with real flower arrangements, you need to incorporate filler flowers into your ribbonwork. These ribbon blooms can be substitutes for buttercups, pink cherry blossoms, apple blossoms, red geraniums, or simply little fantasy flowers. Use wired or unwired ribbons and try mixing and layering them for different looks. The **u-gather technique** is best for these mini flowers.

Simple Fantasy or Filler Flowers

1. Make a simple fantasy or filler flower from a single u-gather of 1/4″ wide x 2″-3″ long ribbon, 1/2″ wide x 4″-5″ long ribbon, or 3/4″ wide x 5″-7″ long ribbon. The longer the ribbon, the fuller the flower.

The single u-gather technique makes a variety of smaller filler flowers for your compositions. Try a double layer for a different look.

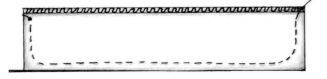

2. Stitch a u-gather in the ribbon and gather to a length of 1/4″. Secure the gathering. Join the ends together by overlapping the ribbon at the first and last stitches and securing.
3. Cover the center with beads or insert stamens.

Cherry Blossoms, Apple Blossoms, Buttercups

This spray of apple blossoms is stitched with continuous u-gathers and narrow ribbon.

1. These blossoms are made from a 4-petal continuous u-gather with 5″-6″ lengths of 1/2″-wide ribbon, or 6″-8″ lengths of 3/4″-wide ribbon. The longer the ribbon, the fuller the petal. If you bunch several blossoms together, you can create geraniums, hydrangeas, and other multi-floret flowers. Unwired silk ribbon will make soft free-form petals, while wired ribbon yields petals with edges that can be shaped.

2. Stitch the u-gather pattern, gather the ribbon tightly, and secure the thread. Insert the stamens.

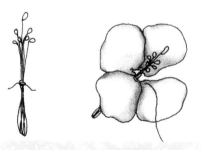

FASHIONING SECRET

Several years ago I was decorating a hat with tiny blue four-petal blossoms. After several frustrating attempts to gather the entire ribbon in one step, I discovered that if I gathered each petal and secured it before going on to the next section, the final result was a much better flower.

3. With the gathered ribbon ends right sides together, stitch the beginning stitch to the last stitch. The center should be quite tight. If not, weave the thread back and forth across the middle, catching the ribbon in the folds near the center's edge until the center is tightly closed.

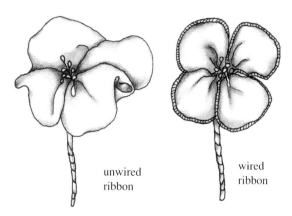

unwired ribbon

wired ribbon

4. If not using stamens, cover the center of the flower with a bead or seed beads. For flowers that have stamens but are not stemmed, coil the stamen ends flat in the back and stitch. Then stitch to crinoline.

Stems

5. To stem flowers with stamens, glue 32-gauge wire alongside the extended stamen ends on the underside of the flower.

6. Cover the stem and any raw edges with floral tape.

Forget-Me-Nots

Stitched forget-me-nots also work well as filler flowers but are best suited for projects that are stitched directly to crinoline.

1. Using embroidery thread, perle cotton, or embroidery silk ribbon, make a series of five French knots in a tight circle. The center of the flower is a yellow French knot (refer to instructions on page 16).

Canterbury Bells

Canterbury bells, as featured in the Woodland Nest project on page 78, are pretty flowers that can be showcased individually or mixed with other flowers. Each stem of bells has three or four open florets and three or four buds. Each floret is stemmed with 32-gauge wire then wrapped in floral tape and added to the main stem of 20-gauge wire. Note the green wire stamen in each bell, which is also the wire used to stem the floret.

It's good to mix colors for this flower. Select wired ombre ribbons 1½″-wide in the lavender and pink ranges. I particularly like the lavender/green and purple/mauve ribbons that were used in the Woodland Nest.

The **tube technique** *is used to make Canterbury bells. Cut 3″ lengths for the buds and 4″ lengths for the bells. Decide which color you want at the bottom edge of the bell and remove the wire on the opposite edge.*

Canterbury bells are made using the tube technique and two different ombre ribbons.

Open Bells

1. Make a tube (refer to page 20 for instructions).
2. Stitch around the top of the tube. Before tightening, attach a piece of wire to the bell as shown.

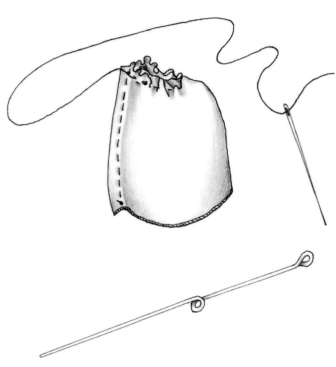

Buds

6. Follow the directions for open bells, except omit the stitching around the bottom of the bell. Instead, squeeze the edges closed, giving it an elongated pleated look.
7. Finish the stems with floral tape.

Assembly

8. To assemble one stem of Canterbury bells, start with a closed bud at the top of the main stem. Secure it by wrapping it with floral tape, then add the remaining buds and the florets in the same way.
9. Style the bells as shown in the photo. The secret to styling these flowers is pinching the wired edge in five places so the edges flare out.

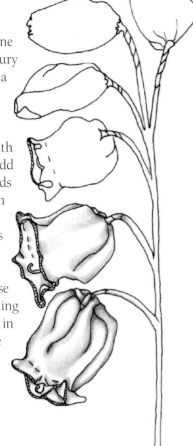

3. Tighten the gathering and stitch the wire stem at the top. Secure the thread and turn right side out.
4. To finish the bell, stitch around the bottom of the floret about 3/16″ from the edge. Loosely gather this into a bell shape and secure the stitching.
5. Wrap the stem with floral tape.

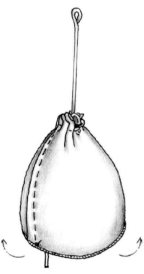

Bluebells

My version of bluebells has two open bells and one closed bell at the top. The technique is the same as for Canterbury bells, except using a piece of blue wired ribbon 1″ wide x 2½″ long for each bell. If you use white or cream ribbon in a width narrower than 1″, they become lilies of the valley!

These bluebells are made like Canterbury bells using the tube technique. Stemmed and wired together, the bluebells make a perfect filler flower for small posies.

Open Bell

1. For each open bell, make a tube and gather the top edge just as you did for the Canterbury bells. Before tightening, glue or stitch a looped 3″ wire stem to the top of the inside of the flower.

2. Tighten the gathering, secure, and turn the tube right side out. The stem wire should be at the top of the bell.

3. Stitch around the bottom of the bell, about 3/16″ from the edge and gently tighten until the bell forms a round shape. Secure the thread and cut.

4. Glue a green or peach stamen in the bell.

Closed Bell

5. The closed bell is made the same way as the open bell, except there is no stamen and no stitching around the bottom of the ribbon. Just crimp it closed.

Assembly

6. Assemble the two open bells and one closed bell together by holding them in position with your fingertips. Wrap all with floral tape or silk thread. They look particularly sweet with their heads bowed.

Berries and Rose Hips

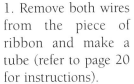

1. Remove both wires from the piece of ribbon and make a tube (refer to page 20 for instructions).

2. Gather the top edge and stitch or glue a 3″ piece of 32-gauge wire to the top of the tube shape. Tighten the gathering and secure.

wire loop

3. Turn right side out (the wire should be at the top). Stuff the bell with a small piece of cotton wadding and stitch around the bottom of the bell, about 1/16″ from the edge.

4. Gather tightly to close the berry, secure, and cut the thread.

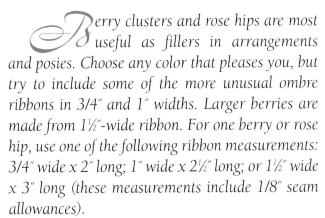

Three ribbon widths are used in these berries ~ 1½″, 1″, and 3/4″. They are shown larger than actual size.

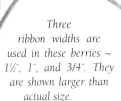

*B*erry clusters and rose hips are most useful as fillers in arrangements and posies. Choose any color that pleases you, but try to include some of the more unusual ombre ribbons in 3/4″ and 1″ widths. Larger berries are made from 1½″-wide ribbon. For one berry or rose hip, use one of the following ribbon measurements: 3/4″ wide x 2″ long; 1″ wide x 2½″ long; or 1½″ wide x 3″ long (these measurements include 1/8″ seam allowances).

If you've made the Canterbury bells, you'll see that berries have many similarities, since they are both made using the **tube technique.**

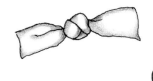

Hollyhocks look wonderful when made with ombre ribbons.

$\mathcal{A}$ true cottage garden flower, these stately tall flowers can be found in a rainbow of colors ranging from white to peach to yellow to pink to claret. Petals can be the old-fashioned singles or the newer double ruffles.

This version of the hollyhock is based on the single floret made using the **tube technique** with 1½"-wide ribbon. The center of each floret is a simple knotted piece of yellow ribbon either 1" or 1½"-wide. The leaves are made from 1½"-wide green ombre ribbon using the **u-gather technique.**

If you plan to stem your flowers, you'll need 32-gauge and 20-gauge covered stem wire and green floral tape.

Hollyhock stems each have three large florets, two medium florets (one open and one closed), and three buds. There are five leaves to each stem ~ two small and three large.

Centers

1. Cut a 3" length of 1½"-wide yellow ribbon. Remove both wires. Tie a knot in the center of the ribbon.

2. Bring the tails down together and glue a 2" piece of 32-gauge stem wire under the knot and between the top of the tails of the ribbon.

Florets

3. Cut three 7½" lengths of 1½"-wide ribbon for the large florets and two 6" lengths for the medium florets. Remove one wire from each piece (this is the gathering edge).

4. Make a tube from each piece of ribbon.

5. Trim the seamed edge and seal it with Fray Check if desired. Finger press the seam to one side.

6. Stitch and gather the top edge but do not tighten.

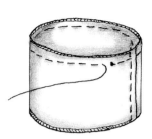

Insert the stemmed yellow center into the middle of the floret so the knot is in the front of the flower and the tails are hidden in the back. Pull the floret gathering tight and secure.

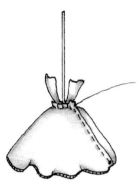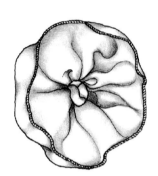

7. Stitch through all the layers to secure the yellow center to the floret. Secure the thread and cut.

8. Trim the excess ribbon, cover the back of the floret, and stem with floral tape.

Bud

9. Cut a 3″ length of ribbon for each bud. Remove both wires and make a tube.

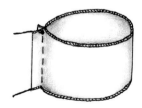

10. Stitch around the top, gather tightly, and turn inside out.

11. Fill with stuffing and gather around the bottom but do not tighten.

12. Stitch or glue a 2″ piece of 32-gauge wire to the inside of the bud. *Note:* Keep one bud unstemmed and glue it directly to the top of the main stem, then tighten the gathering.

13. Tighten and secure the gathering.

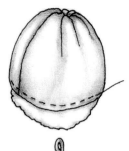

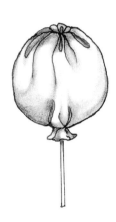

14. Wrap the bottom of the bud and stem wire with floral tape.

Leaves

15. Cut three 6″ lengths and two 4″ lengths of 1½″-wide green wired ribbon. This is enough for the leaves on one stem of hollyhocks.

16. Refer to the stemmed **u-gather** leaves instructions on page 51 and make five leaves.

Assembly

17. Attach all the buds, florets, and leaves to the main stem. Begin with the bud on top and work your way down the stem, adding buds with floral tape. Position the smaller leaves near the top and middle of the hollyhock stem and the large leaves near the bottom. Continue down the stem with florets, small leaves, more florets, and larger leaves, each secured with floral tape.

Fuchsias

$\mathcal{F}$uchsias are a great choice to add a delicate element to your flower compositions. A single bloom can be very elegant, especially in tones of white or cream and with a beaded stem. For something livelier, a cluster of colored fuchsias is full of movement as it wiggles and dangles at the back of a hat.

There are two versions of this flower: the simple faux fuchsia with no central stamen or underskirt, and the frilly full fuchsia loaded with stamens. For practice, start with a 1½"-wide ribbon (it's easier to work with) and then try a 1"-wide ribbon in a variety of colors.

Fuchsias can be made with wired or unwired ribbons, but the wired ones will give you a little more flexibility when styling the finished flower. Try both types to see what works best for you.

The four outer petals for a small fuchsia are made from a 3½" length of 1"-wide ribbon. The large fuchsia has outer petals made from a 5¼" length of 1½"-wide ribbon. Use a 7" length of 1/2"- or 3/4"-wide unwired ribbon or embroidery silk ribbon for the frilly under-skirt (best suited for the larger fuchsia) or fold a sheer 1½"-wide organdy ribbon lengthwise for a double frill.

Stamen colors can be gold, pearl, burgundy, pink, cream, or white ~ the choice is yours.

Fuchsia stems can be lengths of gold thread, beading thread, embroidery thread, or perle cotton. Since some of the beads have to fit over thread that might be too thick for the bead hole, your choice of thread may be somewhat limited.

Faux Fuchsia

The faux fuchsia has only four petals, no underskirt, and no central stamen. Try beading the stems when incorporating them into collage brooches.

1. Fold the ribbon for the outer petals (1″ wide x 3½″ long or 1½″ x 5¼″) and overlap the raw edges in the center.

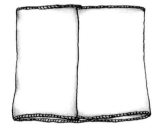

2. Stitch three or four double-headed stamens to the center or near the edge of the folded ribbon, depending on what size ribbon you are using.

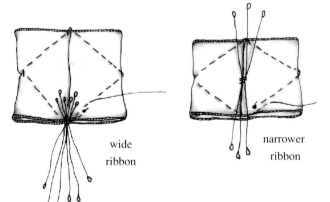

wide ribbon   narrower ribbon

3. Stitch a diamond pattern as illustrated, being sure to go over the edges with the thread for tightly gathered edges.

4. Pull the gathering tight so the four petals spring out, then secure the thread on the underside of the flower so no bulky stitches show.

5. Triple knot the end of a piece of decorative thread and insert it from the underside up into the bulbous cavity at the top of the flower, drawing the needle and thread through to the outside. Cut the thread, leaving a 12″ tail, and set aside until you decide how the fuchsia will be used in your project.

6. Style the flower by fluffing out the four outer petals.

Frilly Fuchsia

1. For the upper petals, overlap the raw edges of a 1½″ wide x 5¼″ long piece of ribbon.

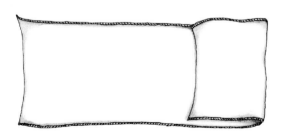

2. With the overlapped edges in the center, stitch the diamond pattern. Go over the edges with the thread for tightly gathered edges. Set aside without gathering, securing, or cutting the thread.

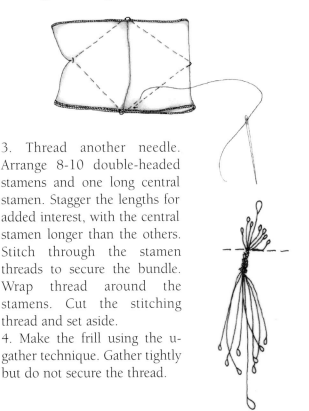

3. Thread another needle. Arrange 8-10 double-headed stamens and one long central stamen. Stagger the lengths for added interest, with the central stamen longer than the others. Stitch through the stamen threads to secure the bundle. Wrap thread around the stamens. Cut the stitching thread and set aside.

4. Make the frill using the u-gather technique. Gather tightly but do not secure the thread.

5. Position the frill around the stamens so no stitches can be seen from under the skirt (think of a ballerina in a short tutu). Adjust the gathering to fit around the stamens, secure it, and join the ends together. Do not cut the thread.

6. Secure the frill to the stamens with a few stitches through the stump of the stamens and the gathered edge of the frill.

7. Clean up the ribbon "hairs" by wrapping thread around the stump. Trim the top of the stump, leaving about 1/4″. Cut the thread.

8. Tack the frill with attached stamens to the lower edge of the upper petal ribbon you already stitched.

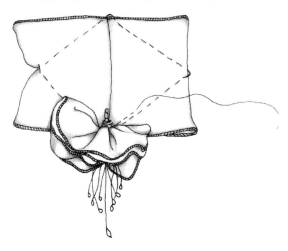

9. Draw in the gathering, being sure the stump of the frill with stamens is covered by the bulbous cavity of the top petals (imagine an old-fashioned nightcap covering a pointy head). Tighten the gathering and secure both the gathering and the frill with several stitches through all the layers of ribbon and stump.

10. Thread a new needle with decorative thread, triple knot the end, and insert it into the underside of the frilly fuchsia, drawing the thread up and out the top of the flower. Leave about 12″ of thread until you decide how the flower will be used. Embellish the thread with some beads if desired. Fluff out the petals and the underskirt.

Chrysanthemums

*his flower is made up entirely of narrow ribbons formed into **knotted loops** and is very easy to construct. Choose ribbons that are approximately 1/4″ to 1/2″ wide in a variety of textures, styles, and coordinated colors. Experiment with embroidery silk ribbons, cotton tape, organdy, variegated and rayon ribbons. Chrysanthemums look lovely on hats and as package decorations.*

1. For a chrysanthemum 4″ in diameter, use seven different ribbons. Cut nine 5½″ lengths of each ribbon, keeping the colors separate. For an even fuller flower, use nine different ribbons and cut 12 5½″ lengths.

2. Tie a knot in the center of each piece of ribbon. Keep the ribbon color groups separate.

3. Arrange the ribbon groups in a row in the color sequence of your choice (this will be the order you stitch them). Start with a knotted ribbon from the first group. Fold it in half so the ends meet and the knot is at the bottom of the loop. Secure the thread with a few backstitches, then stitch two small running stitches across the top edge of the loop petal about 1/4″ from the top.

4. Select a ribbon from the second group and stitch two running stitches across its top edge. Slide the ribbon along the thread so it is next to the first petal.

5. Repeat with a ribbon from the third group.

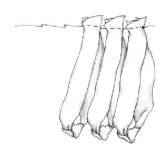

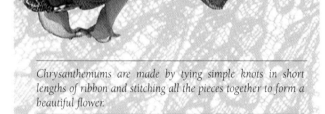

Chrysanthemums are made by tying simple knots in short lengths of ribbon and stitching all the pieces together to form a beautiful flower.

6. Thread on all the ribbons, repeating the sequence until all are hanging from the thread. (The mental image I have at this stage is one of clothes hanging on a line.) Be careful to keep the string of threaded ribbons untwisted.

7. When all the pieces are on the thread, push the ribbons together so they are tightly gathered. Secure the gathering, then roll it into the finished chrysanthemum. *Note:* Stitch through all the layers so the center of the flower doesn't pop up. One way to make sure the center is secure is to stitch the ribbon roll as you go.

Delphiniums

Bias cut silk ribbon in a variety of blues defines these blossoms as delphiniums. Each stem has approximately 20 florets.

Delphiniums are wonderful when made from bias cut silk ribbon in a range of blues. Make several of these flowers and use them in large floral arrangements, twig bowers, wreaths, or as a simple bouquet to sit on a dresser or shelf. I have taken some liberty with this flower regarding its size and shape so you may see similarities to larkspur. If you want larkspur in your composition, use pale pink and off-white ribbon instead of the blues I have chosen.

Each flower stem is an 18″ length of 20-gauge stem wire and has 20-25 florets, with each floret made up of two 1½″-wide bias cut silk ribbon squares with stamen centers. If you're making one stem and mixing two colors, you will need one yard of each color. The dark blue stem is a mix of dark blue and medium purple ribbon, the medium blue stem is a mix of dusty blue and medium purple, and the light blue stem is pale lavender/blue.

For each dark blue floret, you'll need three black double-headed stamens and for each medium and light blue floret, you'll need three white double-headed stamens.

1. Offset two 1½″ x 1½″ pieces of ribbon as shown. Make a tiny slit in the center.

2. Fold over the stamens so all the heads are together, wrap the center of the stamens with thread, and insert them into the slit in the silk ribbon. The stamens should protrude approximately 3/8″ above the slit in the ribbon.

3. Place a dot of glue at the junction of the stamens and the ribbon and pinch them together at the base.

4. Wrap the exposed stamen stem with floral tape.
5. Make 20-25 florets in the same manner.

Assembly

6. Assemble the flowers, starting with one floret at the top of the stem wire. Wrap with floral tape and continue adding florets until they are all secured. The florets will cover about 8″ of the stem.

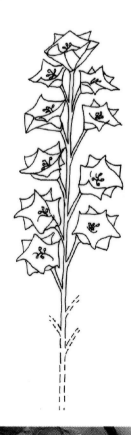

Carnations

$\mathcal{W}$ith their unique spicy yet sweet perfume, carnations are a favorite of most florists. They will be your favorite too when you see how simple they are to make.

Using bias cut silk ribbons, these make up into gorgeous fluffy flowers when stitched with the **straight stitch pattern**. They work well as a stemmed flower in arrangements or bowers and look very pretty as an accent flower on a hat.

Pale cream ribbon with pink tinted edges shows off the carnation to perfection. You will need 18″-24″ of 1″-wide bias cut silk ribbon or 36″-40″ of 1½″-wide. The length depends on how full you want the flower.

1. Begin the flower by fraying the top edge of the ribbon using your first finger and thumb. Stitch across the bottom of the ribbon about 1/16″ from the edge and gather to a length of about 1″. Secure the gathering.

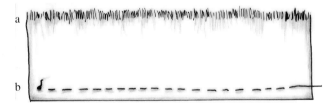

2. Roll up the gathered ribbon, stitching through all the layers as you go.

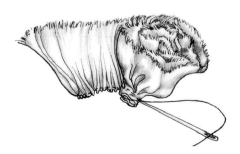

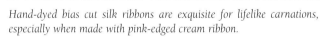

Hand-dyed bias cut silk ribbons are exquisite for lifelike carnations, especially when made with pink-edged cream ribbon.

3. Stitch to crinoline or if stemming the flower, insert and glue an 18″ piece of 20-gauge stem wire into the base of the flower.

4. Wrap the stem wire with floral tape, being sure to cover all the raw edges of ribbon.

Peonies

The red peony has frayed outer petals, while the claret one has smooth petals. Both flowers are the Quick Peony.

Quick Peony

1. Cut one 36″ length and nine 8″ lengths from three yards of 2½″-wide ribbon. With your thumb and first finger, fray the tops of the long piece and four of the 8″ pieces. The remaining five pieces can be left plain or frayed. The samples on this page show both.

2. **Row 1:** With very sharp scissors, make 1/2″ deep snips in the frayed edge of the 36″ length at approximately 1/4″ intervals.

3. Using the straight stitch pattern, gather only the lower edge of the ribbon about 1/8″ from the edge of the ribbon. Tighten the gathering to approximately 4″ long, but don't secure.

4. At this point I recommend practicing rolling up the ribbon until it's gathered enough for the base to be tight, but with the top fluffy and loose. Experiment a little and adjust the gathering as needed. When satisfied, secure the gathering and roll up the gathered ribbon with stitches through all the layers. If it's secure enough, the flower shouldn't come up when you give it a gentle tug in the center.

5. Stitch the base of the flower to a 2″ circle of crinoline (it will look like a teacup on a miniature saucer) and set aside.

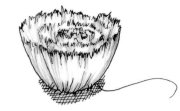

Peonies are often bigger than some roses and as such are fabulous alternative flowers for very large picture hats. With a 2½″-wide silk ribbon, you can create a peony that is approximately 6″ in diameter.

There are two types of peonies you can make ~ a quick peony or a fancy variation ~ and the instructions for both are given.

Bias cut satin silk ribbon is the ribbon of choice for this flower since the edges don't unravel like woven ribbon and the satin gives a lustrous quality to the finished peony. The techniques used are **straight gather** and **u-gather**. Colors are strictly your choice ~ try taupe or soft pink, a claret or hot red. Gold tones or luscious creams are also stunning.

6. **Row 2:** Stitch each of the nine 8″ lengths of ribbon with the single u-gather technique to make individual petals. *Note:* The frayed edge is the top of the petal. Gather each to a length of about 1/2″. Set aside the five unfrayed petals.

7. Pin the four frayed petals evenly around the base of the flower center (they may overlap). Stitch these to the crinoline very close to the base of the central part of the flower. Remove the pins but don't cut the thread.

8. **Row 3:** Evenly overlap, pin, and stitch the remaining five petals to the crinoline close to the previous row of petals. Remove the pins, secure the stitches, and cut the thread.

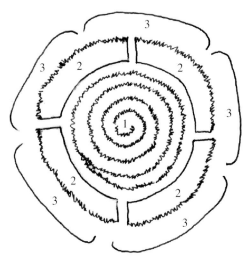

9. Before you apply the peony to your project, trim any excess crinoline and cover the back with ribbon or felt. A pin back stitched to the backing will make the flower removable.

Leaves

10. Make three boat leaves (page 52) with 4″ lengths of 1½″-wide ribbon folded lengthwise. The leaves can be stemmed or simply stitched under the flower.

Fancy Peony

For this peony, use bias cut silk ribbons in two colors and two widths: From 1½″-wide **creamy pink** ribbon, cut one 30″ length and one 25″ length. From 1½″-wide **pale pink** ribbon, cut two 20″ lengths. From 2½″-wide **pale pink** ribbon, cut six 2″ lengths and five 9″ lengths.

1. **Row 1:** Begin the peony center by fraying the top of the 30″ piece of creamy pink ribbon. Straight gather it on the bottom edge to a length of 3″. Secure the gathering.

Roll up the gathering and secure with stitches through all the layers. If it's secure, the flower shouldn't come up when you give it a gentle tug in the center. Stitch to a 2″ circle of crinoline at the base.

2. **Row 2:** Fray the top edge of one of the 20″ pale pink lengths, then make 1/4″ deep snips at 1/8″ intervals (don't bother to measure, just estimate). Divide the

ribbon into five 4″ sections and mark each section with a crease. Stitch a continuous 5-petal u-gather (one u-gather per section).

Gather and position the continuous petals around the flower center to make sure it will encircle the center completely. Secure the gathering and stitch the petals to crinoline at the base of the flower center.

3. **Row 3:** Repeat Row 2 with the 25″ piece of creamy pink ribbon, making the u-gather sections 5″ instead of 4″. Gather and position slightly offset to Row 2. Stitch the petals to the crinoline very close to the rest of the flower.

4. **Row 4:** Fray the top edge of the remaining 20″ piece of pale pink ribbon and straight gather it into a ruffle sized to fit around the last row of petals. Stitch in place on the crinoline. Trim the excess crinoline to within 1/8″ and set aside.

Note: The next two rows are executed in reverse order (do Row 6 before Row 5). This is not a typographical error!

5. **Row 6:** Cut a new 2″ circle of crinoline. Stitch each of the five 9″ pale pink lengths into single u-gather petals and gather tightly. Evenly arrange the petals and stitch in place about 1/4″ from the edge of the crinoline circle.

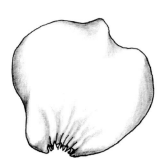

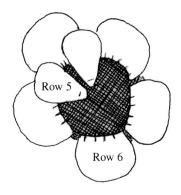

6. **Row 5:** Round the top corners of the six 2″ lengths of pale pink ribbon by trimming with scissors. Pleat the bottom of each petal. Evenly arrange on top of and slightly in from the outer edge of the last row of petals

and stitch to the crinoline circle. You should only be able to see about 1″ diameter of crinoline in the center now.

7. Stitch the center section you have set aside from Row 4 on top of Row 5 and Row 6. If there are gaps between the rows, tack the petals down in inconspicuous places.

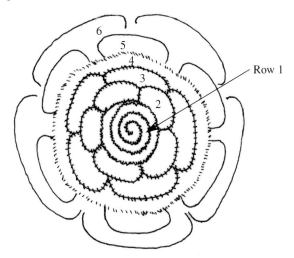

8. Cover the crinoline and raw edges on the back of the peony with ribbon, felt, or Ultrasuede.

Leaves

9. Make five stemmed boat leaves (page 52) from five 4½″ lengths of 2″-wide pale green wired ribbon, folded lengthwise.

10. Cut five 8″ lengths of 32-gauge stem wire. Stitch these to the back of the leaf, then wrap the stems with perle cotton or silk embroidery thread in a color to match the leaf.

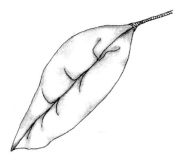

Gardenias

Gardenias are most believable when the centers are tight and the outer petals are wide open and twisted a half turn.

I love gardenias ~ they remind me of my parents' garden in Epping, Australia. When I visit, my father often greets me at the airport with a gardenia. The perfume is intoxicating. Pure joy ~ both in the gardenia's fragrance and in seeing Dad! If you are not familiar with the gardenia, go to your local nursery and immerse yourself in its exotic perfume. Lucky are you readers who can grow gardenias.

This ribbon version of the gardenia has only ten petals ~ five **dipped corner petals** for the inside and five **rolled corner petals** for the outside. These stunning creamy white flowers can be used as corsages, on hats and purses, as package decorations, and as beautiful adornments to a pure white tea cozy. They are particularly elegant decorations for a wedding cake.

1. Cut five 2½" lengths of 1½"-wide ribbon for the dipped corner petals and five 3" lengths for the rolled corner petals.

five dipped corner petals
(inner)

five rolled corner petals
(outer)

2. Refer to the instructions on pages 18-19 to make the petals using the ribbon measurements above. Keep the dipped corner petals separate from the rolled corner petals.

3. Overlap the five dipped corner petals by approximately 1/2 and stitch these inner petals together in a row.

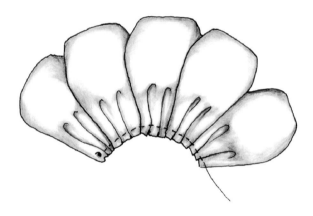

Roll them up tightly and secure them with stitches through the stump (base of the flower).

4. Working clockwise, evenly position each rolled corner petal on the base of the inner petals, overlapping about 1/3 or less. Stitch all five petals in place.

FASHIONING SECRET

To avoid a rose-looking gardenia, style the inner petals tightly together (they should not unfurl too much). Then simply twist the outer petals 1/2 turn.

twist each petal
1/2 turn

Stems

5. Add stems by making a hole through the base of the flower and inserting a 22-gauge wire into the hole. Secure it with a dot of glue.

6. Cover the back with a dark green calyx (tube technique) and wrap the stem with silk thread or perle cotton.

Leaves

7. To enhance the purity of these blooms, make three boat leaves from solid dark green ribbon 1" wide x 5" long, folded widthwise (refer to instructions on page 52). Stem the leaves and wrap the stem wire with perle cotton or silk thread.

Leaves

Gathered Prairie Point Leaves

1. Use ribbon 1½″ wide x 3½″ long or 1″ wide x 2½″ long. Fold the ribbon ends down as shown. Remove the bottom wire.

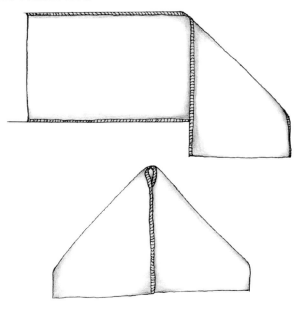

2. Stitch across the bottom, being sure to catch all the ribbon on the back in the stitching.

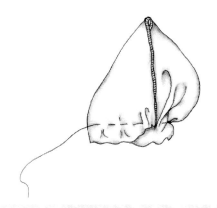

*A*ll flowers need a little greenery! Experiment with a green bow, a piece of scrunched up ribbon, a spray of millinery leaves, or some lovely stitched ribbon leaves. Some compositions require dozens of leaves, while others need only two or three. If your composition has several different flowers, try a variety of leaf styles in different colors.

Following are several stitched leaf techniques with their basic ribbon measurements. When making leaves for a specific project, use the ribbon measurements given in the project to make the leaves.

Make up several of each leaf, following the illustrations for each style. Be forewarned ~ you will need lots of leaves for ribbonwork, so it's a good idea to make up a "bag o' leaves" and store them until needed.

FASHIONING SECRET

Ombre ribbons are a great choice for leaves because you have two colors in one. Remember, not all leaves are green. Try adding a pink, mauve, or autumn-toned leaf to your design to see what happens. An accent leaf can also work wonders for your design. Try a metallic silver, gold, or copper ribbon, a striped ribbon, or a wired sheer ribbon for a little pizzazz.

3. Gather very tightly, then wrap the thread around the base two or three times and secure (I call this "choking" the stump with thread). Trim the ends.

4. Prairie point leaves can be stitched directly to your project or stemmed by gluing a piece of 32-gauge wire into the base of the leaf. Wrap with floral tape, perle cotton, or silk thread.

Pleated Prairie Point Leaves

1. Use ribbon 1½″ wide x 3½″ long or 1″ wide x 2½″ long. Fold the same as the gathered version, except with two sets of pleats ~ one on the right side and one on the left.

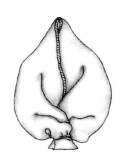

2. Stitch the bottom to secure the pleats, then "choke" the stump by wrapping the thread around it very tightly. Secure the thread, cut, and trim the ends.

3. Prairie point leaves can be stitched directly to your project or stemmed by gluing a piece of 32-gauge wire into the base of the leaf. Wrap with floral tape, perle cotton, or silk thread.

U-Gathered Leaves

1. Use 1½″-wide ribbon in any of the following lengths, depending on the size leaf you need: 4″, 5″, 6″, or 8″.

2. Gather tightly. U-gathered leaves can be stemmed by gluing or stitching a 2″ piece of 32-gauge wire to the gathered edge of the ribbon.

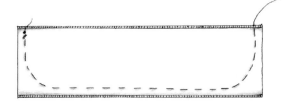

3. Cover the raw edges and stems with floral tape. U-gathered leaves are perfect for hollyhocks.

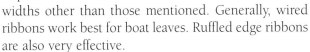

Boat Leaves

Many different leaf shapes can be made from this one stitch pattern. Experiment with ribbon widths other than those mentioned. Generally, wired ribbons work best for boat leaves. Ruffled edge ribbons are also very effective.

These leaves are good with gardenias, pansies, peonies, and roses. They can be stitched directly to your project or stemmed by stitching 32-gauge wire to the back seam of the leaf. Wrap the raw ends and stem with thread, ribbon, or floral tape.

Make a sample from each of the following lengths. Label and keep them handy for reference.

❋ 8″-10″ of 1½″-wide ribbon folded in half widthwise
❋ 5″ of 1″-wide ribbon folded in half widthwise
❋ 2½″-4″ of 1½″-wide ribbon folded in half lengthwise
❋ 4½″ of 2″-wide ribbon folded in half lengthwise

Boat Leaves Folded Widthwise

fold

1. Remove the bottom wire and fold up the corners. Stitch along the fold from one point, down the sloping side, along the bottom edge of the "boat," and up the other slope.

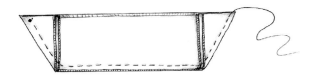

2. Gather the ribbon until the bottom of the boat shape disappears into a straight line. Do not secure.

3. Open up the ribbon and adjust the gathering as desired. Secure and trim any loose threads and ribbon.

4. Style the leaf by pushing the ribbon from the folded point toward the middle.

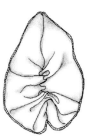

Boat Leaves Folded Lengthwise

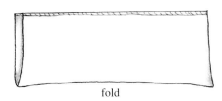

fold

1. Do not remove the wires. Turn up each bottom corner and make a few stitches across the top of the wired edges on one point. *Note:* For a neater point, fold the left raw edge of the ribbon in 1/2″ before turning up the bottom left corner.

2. Stitch along the fold from the point, down the sloping side, along the bottom fold of the "boat," and up the other slope.

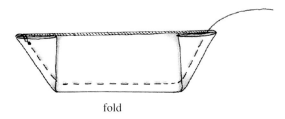

fold

3. Gather the ribbon until the bottom of the boat shape disappears into a straight line. Do not secure.

4. Open up the ribbon and adjust the gathering as desired. Secure and trim any loose threads and ribbon.

5. Style the leaf by pushing the ribbon from one point toward the middle.

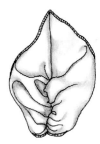

Mitered Leaves

Mitered leaves work well with cabochon roses or when applied to crinoline-based compositions because their tails are folded under and hidden by the leaf.

1. Fold a 4½″ length of 1½″-wide or a 3″ length of 1″-wide ribbon in half.

2. Turn down one corner and stitch across the fold. Secure the thread.

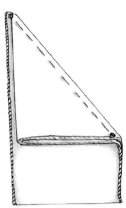

3. Open up the ribbon.

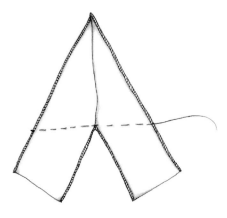

4. Stitch across the width of both sides of the ribbon.

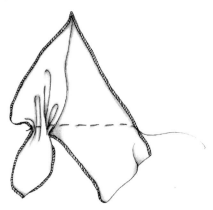

5. Gather tightly and secure the thread. Trim the tails and tuck them under the leaf. Trim off the loose ribbon flap in the back of the leaf.

An assortment of ribbon colors and leaf styles are combined to create this fabulous leaf collage.

Calyx

The calyx is the small green cap at the base of most flowers. In nature it holds the flower petals together and in ribbonwork it covers all the raw edges. On some stemmed ribbon flowers the base and stem are wrapped in floral tape, while on others they're wrapped in ribbon or thread. An alternative for stemmed flowers is a ribbon calyx (tube technique) around the base of the flower.

1. Remove both wires from the ribbon and make a tube.

2. With right sides out, slip the tube up the stem. Position it so all the raw edges of the petals are covered, then slipstitch in place.
3. Wrap the thread around the excess ribbon and stem. Secure and cut the thread.

For a non-stemmed flower such as a cabochon rose bud that will be sewn to crinoline, make the calyx from narrower ribbon wrapped around the base of the bud. Stitch it in place and tuck the ends under the bud.

Stems

Wire Stems

1. Wrap wire stems with floral tape, bias silk ribbon, embroidery thread, silk thread, or perle cotton. Refer to the instructions for thread wrap on page 20.

Ribbon Stems

1. To make the stem tube, cut a 6″ length of 1″-wide bias cut silk ribbon. Refer to the tube technique described on page 20.
2. Stems that will be stitched to crinoline or other flat surfaces can be made by twisting a length of ribbon. Fold in the raw edges and tightly twist the ribbon. Couch or stitch it to crinoline or fabric.

Chapter 4:
Fashioning Roses

―――◆―――

"I have been ruining myself in black sattin ribbon with a proper perl edge; and now I am trying to draw it up into kinds of roses, instead of putting it in plain double plaits."

Jane Austen, 1814

―――◆―――

These tea roses were made by combining two techniques and four ribbons.

The queen of all flowers–the classic rose in all its splendor

Without question the rose is my favorite flower to grow, paint, and to make from ribbon. My small Colorado garden is home to ten rose bushes that bring me great joy every summer. I have photographed them, videotaped them, and painted them. My sofa and draperies are covered with a pink rose pattern and there are several teapots and teacups sitting in my china hutch with roses on them. Roses represent graciousness and romance. They have been the basis for my ribbon creations and have been truly inspirational.

Following are a variety of ribbon roses including gathered roses, folded roses, and petaled roses such as the wild rose, tea rose, and the sweet little cabochon rose. Some of the roses are simple, while others are more challenging. All, however, will result in beautiful roses and some will seem so life-like you'll be tempted to sniff them. The different techniques used to make the roses are **gathered, folded, dipped corner petals, rolled corner petals,** and **u-gathered petals.** Review these techniques in the Techniques section beginning on page 16.

As you read the rose-making instructions, you will see that I sometimes use a combination of techniques to make one rose. For example, I might use a folded center with dipped petals, a folded center with both u-gather and rolled petals, or stamen centers with multiple u-gather petals followed by larger u-gathered petals and rolled petals. Notice that some roses also have blended ribbon combinations which include sheers, solids, ombres, stripes, and velvet. Roses can be made from a variety of ribbon widths from 3/4″ to 2″ or wider.

Gathered Roses

A small gathered rose, a few leaves, and loops of satin cord are combined in a gold filigree pin. Wear it on a blouse with a lace or delicately crocheted handkerchief.

*This is the simplest rose to make using the **gathering technique** stitched or gathered on the wire. It can be made with any width of ribbon and in a variety of lengths. Practice with 1½"-wide ribbon until you become proficient. By combining several of these charming roses in different colors or adding leaves, you can quickly make a brooch or hair ornament.*

Start with an 18"-24" length of 1½"-wide wired ribbon for gathering on the wire or when using the u-gather stitch pattern. If making the smaller rose (like the one in the brooch), you'll need an 8"-10" length of 1½"-wide wired ribbon.

Wire Technique

1. Expose 1/2" of the two wires on one end of the ribbon and twist them together. Starting at the other end, gather the ribbon along one wire only and push it toward the secured end.

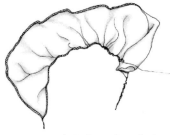

2. When tightly gathered, secure by twisting the other wires together. Fold one end down (long enough to have a scrap of ribbon to hold onto) and stitch in place.

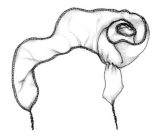

3. Roll the stump the full length of the gathered ribbon.

4. Make a few stitches to secure the rolls as you go. Complete the rose by folding down the raw edge and stitching it securely at the base of the rose.
5. Trim the excess ribbon and wire. The rose can be stemmed or stitched to crinoline.

U-Gather Technique

1. Remove one wire before stitching as shown.

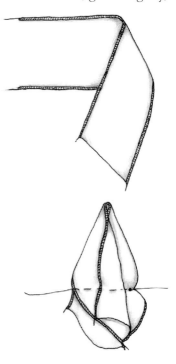

2. Gather the ribbon, fold one end over, and roll up all the gathering just as you did for the wire technique. Stitch as you go.

3. Bring the tail of the ribbon to the base of the stump and stitch through all the layers to secure. You can now stitch the rose to crinoline or stem it.

FASHIONING SECRET

For a different look, style the rose by turning back the top edge of the ribbon as you are rolling it.

Flat Rosebuds

This small, flat rosebud is made from ribbon 1/2″ or 1″ wide x 2″ long and is best suited for flat compositions. Try a length of 2½″ x 1″ wide for the green calyx. Making this little bud is a great way to use up leftover pieces of ribbon.

1. Fold the bud ribbon, gather tightly, and secure.

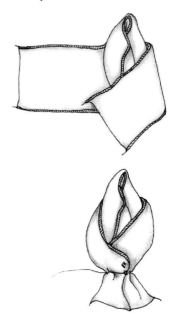

2. Wrap the calyx ribbon around the gathered bud and stitch it in place.

3. Trim the ends and stitch to crinoline or as needed for your project.

Folded Roses

This blended folded rose is made by folding two different ribbons at the same time.

A sheer 3″-wide ribbon was used to make the freeform folded rose above.

The unique ribbon and the twists and crimps to the wired edge make this folded rose stand out from the crowd.

*W*hen you need a rose in a hurry, this is the one to make. It's definitely the quickest rose to make, but is a little tricky to learn. Once you've mastered it though, you'll want to fold every ribbon you see!

It is made from a single length of ribbon using the **folded technique**. Try a few of these with 1½″-wide wired ribbon in a variety of lengths from 12″ to 20″. Sometimes I just start making the rose and cut off the ribbon when I've reached the size I want.

Remember to keep the top of this rose level in order to avoid the dreaded telescoping rose center!

1. Fold down the right end of the ribbon.

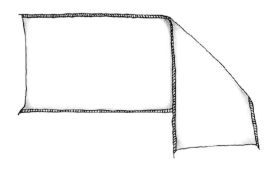

2. Fold the ribbon across once, then roll it five or six times to form a coiled center/stump. These rolls are the secret to beautiful rose centers. Stitch the stump to secure. Do not cut the thread.

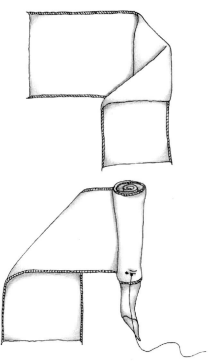

3. Fold back all the ribbon on the left. Tilt the coiled ribbon stump (to add "air" between the folded layers) and roll it across the diagonal fold of the turned back ribbon.

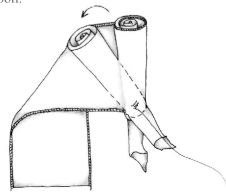

Stitch the stump to secure all the ribbon folds.

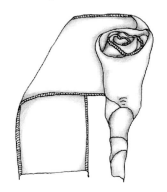

4. Again, fold back all the ribbon on the left, tilt the stump, and roll it across the diagonal fold. Be sure there is plenty of air space for the petals to breath! Secure. Repeat this as many times as needed ~ it can be two or three times for a small to medium rose, or six times or more for a larger rose. Experiment. The worst that can happen is undoing the rose and starting again.

5. To finish, fold the end of the ribbon down and stitch the raw edge into the base of the stump.

6. Trim the excess stump and apply the rose to your project by folding the stump under and stitching the rose in position.

Stems

7. If stemming the rose or using it as the center of a blended rose, glue and insert a wire into the base of the completed flower.

FASHIONING SECRET

Notice how the petals are styled. Too often you see these roses made with no adjustment to the folds in the ribbon ~ the flowers look rather stilted, ordinary, and uninteresting. But pinch and twist the ribbon here and there and the flower takes on a real rose shape! As you look through this book, notice the huge variety in size, color, and style. Experiment with both narrow and wide ribbons. Create a new look by blending two ribbons of the same width (try an ombre and an organdy or wired sheer) at one time to make a single rose.

Wild Roses

With only five petals and some stamens, the wild rose is the simplest of the petaled roses to make.

*T*he wild rose is the easiest petaled rose to make using the **dipped corner petal technique.** With only five petals and a simple center surrounded with stamens, you will be able to make several in an evening.

1. Cut five 3¼″ lengths of 1½″-wide ribbon. Remove both wires and make the petals according to the directions for dipped corner petals on page 18.

2. Glue a small ball of wadding to the top of a 6″ piece of 20-gauge stem wire. Cover it with a 1″-1½″ square of lime green ribbon (wires removed), wrapping thread around it to secure.

3. Position 10-15 double-headed stamens around the green center so they stand up about 1/2″ from the top of the flower center. Secure with thread.

4. Stitch the first petal to the center so the stitching at the base of the petal lines up with the base of the flower center.

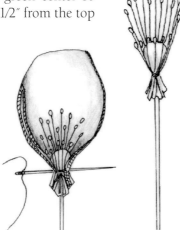

5. Stitch the second petal around the center, overlapping the first petal by 1/3.

6. Continue in this manner until all the petals are stitched on. Style the petals by cupping them with your thumb and first finger.

7. Use the tube technique to make a calyx for the base from a 1″ x 2″ piece of ribbon with both wires removed.

8. Slipstitch the tube (right side out) to the underside of the wild rose. Wrap thread around the stem and the excess ribbon below. Secure the thread.

9. Wrap the stem with floral tape, bias cut silk ribbon, or perle cotton.

FASHIONING SECRET

You can make a variation of the wild rose by substituting the five dipped corner petals for five single u-gathered petals. Stitch the overlapped petals on a crinoline circle. Cover the center with gold thread and an antique button as an alternative to stamens. For an example of this style rose, turn to the Wildwood Brooch project on page 88.

Tea Roses

These are the most beautiful and realistic of all the ribbon roses. They take some time to make but are well worth the effort. To speed up the process, make all the petals ahead of time and sort them into groups according to their cut size. I often make rolled corner petals while watching TV. I make a variety of sizes and colors and store them in plastic baggies ready for use at a later time. I also do this with leaves ~ you can't have too many.

Basic Tea Rose

The basic tea rose with 21 petals and a stamen center. Each petal is made using the rolled corner technique.

The basic tea rose can be enhanced with one or two sheer petals in a coordinating ribbon color.

A student's example of the basic tea rose.

Novel Trimmings Which Make the New Autumn Waists Attractive

Original Designs by M. Louise Walter

Ribbon Roses the Decoration

This fetching waist shows many varying shades of pink. It is a simple tucked shirt-waist model in wild-rose pink louisine silk, trimmed with a floral jabot in front. Shaded pink ribbon roses mingled with green satin leaves are used to make the jabot. The silk bands of the collar and cuffs are cat-stitched in black.

Detail from a page of the Woman's Home Companion, *October 1903, showing ribbon roses decorating the front of a shirt-waist. These would be similar to the basic tea rose.*

If you've made the wild rose, the basic tea rose will be easy for you. You need about three yards of 1½"-wide wired ribbon in a solid, ombre, or crossweave in any color you like. The number of **rolled corner petals** can vary from 13 to 21, so if there's any leftover ribbon you can use it for buds. You will also need 15-20 double-headed stamens in yellow, peach, gold, olive green, or brown for the rose center.

1. Cut 15 3½" lengths and six 4" lengths of 1½"-wide wired ribbon.
2. Refer to the rolled corner petal instructions on page 19 and make 15 petals from the 3½" lengths and six from the 4" lengths. Keep the petal sizes separate.
3. If you intend to stem the rose, twist a piece of 22-gauge wire around the middle of the stamens, fold the stamens in half, wrap them with thread or wire at their base, and stitch them to the first petal. The top of the stamens should come about halfway up the height of the petal.

4. If not stemming the rose, fold the stamens in half, secure with thread around their base, and stitch the bunch to the first petal. The tops of the stamens come about halfway up the height of the petal.

5. Start the rose with three small rolled corner petals. Remember, the rolled corners face away from the center of the rose.

back view

Working clockwise, use the petal with the stamens stitched to it as a base, add a second petal, overlapping the first about halfway.

Stitch the two petals together. Continue with a third petal, overlapping the second.

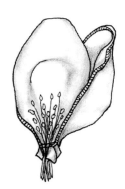

FASHIONING SECRET

Position the smallest petals at the center of the rose and the larger petals on the outside rows. The profile view of the rose shows that the tops of the flower petals are almost all the same height. The longer outer petals will cup the most, thus giving the illusion that all the petals are the same height. Avoid the telescoping rose center!

FASHIONING SECRET

For ease of stitching, hold the rose with your thumb inside the center and the stem at your fingertips.

FASHIONING SECRET

To make a bud, stop adding petals after stitching the third or fourth. If you want a full blown rose, keep going!

6. Working clockwise, continue adding the 12 remaining 3½″ petals, overlapping each by about 1/3. Stitch each petal, checking that it is visible and not completely hidden behind another petal (you may have to adjust the petal spacing a little). From time to time, make a few stitches through the center of the rose stump so that all the petals are secure.

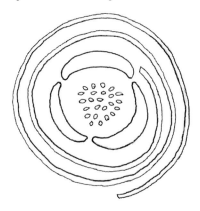

7. Complete the rose by stitching on the six 4″ petals in a clockwise direction, overlapping each by about 1/4.

8. If not stemming the rose, trim the bottom of the stump so the back is relatively flat. Cover all the raw edges of the petals in the back with a piece of folded ribbon. If making a brooch, stitch a pin back to the covering and it's ready to wear.

9. If stemming the rose, cover the raw petal edges by making a green calyx. Make a tube from ribbon 1½″ wide x 2¾″ long. With right sides facing out, slip the tube up the stem and slipstitch the top to the petals. Wrap the bottom of the calyx with thread around the stem. Cover this with floral tape or bias cut silk ribbon, or wrap with perle cotton.

Blended Tea Rose

Several of the roses on these pages are made with blended ribbons and techniques. Look carefully and try to recognize the different techniques used. Blending combinations are almost endless. The pink rose is made up of four ribbons and two techniques ~ a folded rose center and rolled corner petals. The raspberry/yellow rose is made from two ribbons and four techniques ~ a folded rose, single u-gather petals, and dipped and rolled corner petals.

1. The techniques used to make the petals for the cream roses are the **continuous 4-petal u-gather**, the **single u-gather**, and the **rolled corner petal**. Use one yard of 1″-wide peachy pink to cream ombre for the two center rows of the rose and 2¼ yards of 1½″-wide solid cream ribbon for the remaining petals (you may have leftovers).

2. You will need at least 15 double-headed stamens in a mix of red, yellow, gold, and green. Decide if the

rose will be stemmed or not, then bunch the stamens accordingly.

3. Using the ribbon widths and lengths below, make the petals. Group the petals according to row.

continuous 4-petal
u-gather

single u-gather

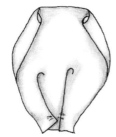

rolled corner petal back view

Row 1: 1 continuous 4-petal u-gather (ombre ribbon 1″ wide x 8½″ long). If desired, add another row of continuous u-gather petals after the first row.

Row 2: 4 single u-gather petals (ombre ribbon 1″ wide x 3½″ long). For taller petals, use 1½″ wide x 4″ long.

Row 3: 5 rolled corner petals (solid ribbon 1½″ wide x 3½″ long).

Row 4: 6 rolled corner petals (solid ribbon 1½″ wide x 4″ long).

Row 5: 7 rolled corner petals (solid ribbon 1½″ wide x 4½″ long).

4. Working clockwise, stitch the first row of petals tightly to the stamen center. All subsequent petals should overlap.

5. When the rose is complete, cover all the raw edges in the back with a piece of folded ribbon as described for the basic tea rose or leave it plain and stitch it directly to crinoline for the composition you're working on. If the rose is stemmed, stitch a tube calyx to the underside of the petals and wrap the stems with floral tape.

Cabochon Roses

This is the sweet little rose so often found on clothes from the early part of this century. There are two different samples of cabochon roses on the 1920's evening dress. The larger rose has eight rolled u-gather petals surrounding a coiled center, while the smaller rose has only three petals. The centers of these roses are usually fastened to a crinoline base.

A small sampling of cabochon rosebuds made from different size ribbons.

1. For the soft pink version of this rose, make three rolled u-gather petals from ombre ribbon 1½″ wide x 2½″ long. Tightly roll down 1/3 of the ribbon width and pin the edges to keep them from unrolling.

2. Sew the u-gather stitch pattern on each petal and gather to a length of about 1/4″ (the petal should cup). Set aside.

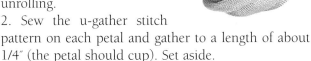

3. Make the center of the rose from a 10″ length of 1/2″-wide ribbon or 13mm silk embroidery ribbon in a color slightly darker than the rose petals (or use 1″-wide ribbon folded in half lengthwise). Using either ribbon, stitch the u-gather pattern 1/8″ from the edge and gather.

4. Coil and stitch the ribbon to a circle of crinoline 3/4″ in diameter. Coil the gathering tightly in the center and more loosely towards the outer edges. Tack down some of the edges of the ribbon to flatten it slightly.

FASHIONING SECRET

I sometimes make the rose center with a small flattened folded rose.

5. With the rolled edge to the outside, slip one of the petals around the circle of crinoline so the gathering is on the underside and the top of the cupped petal encloses part of the coiled center. Secure the petal by stitching the underside of the petal through the crinoline in several places.

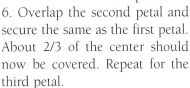

6. Overlap the second petal and secure the same as the first petal. About 2/3 of the center should now be covered. Repeat for the third petal.

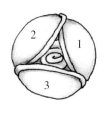

7. Stitch the finished rose to the rest of the composition where needed. To make a smaller rose, use the measurements of the Collage Brooch project on page 70.

Bud and Calyx

A simple rosebud with ribbon calyx and mitered leaves.

8. To make a bud, fold a small piece of ribbon and wrap it with one rolled u-gather petal.

9. For the calyx, wrap ribbon around the base and tuck it behind in the back. Tack the bud to crinoline.

inner fold   wrapped outer petal   calyx

Chapter 5

Heirlooms for the Next Generation

The Ribbonwork Collection

Collage Brooch with Roses and Faux Fuchsias

Collage brooches are one way to use up small pieces of ribbon. This spectacular brooch combines a gathered rose, cabochon rose, faux fuchsias, fantasy filler flowers, leaves, and beads.

*N*estled in the folds of a reproduction 1918 Armistice blouse, this brooch is truly spectacular. It is made up of 10-12 elements arranged as a collage of flowers, lace, loops, stamens, buttons, beads, and leaves. The loops, faux fuchsias, and small cabochon rose are made from 1950's vintage ribbon.

Collages are an excellent way to use all those odds and ends and miscellaneous flowers you made when you didn't have anything specific in mind. Make these collages as brooches, for decorating pillows, or to dress up purses.

WARNING: Beware of kitties! If you have cats, they will be very attracted to the dangling fuchsias. My cat, Wiggy, loves this brooch. How do I know? Because one morning I found it on the floor in a completely disheveled state. Fortunately I was able to repair most of the ribbonwork but the cabochon rose needed to be completely replaced. It didn't even qualify as vintage wear and tear. The tooth mark was just too obvious!

YOU WILL NEED:

Ribbon Flowers & Leaves
large pink rose (page 57)
flat rosebud (page 58)
small cabochon rose (page 66)
2-3 fantasy flowers (page 30)
3 faux fuchsias (page 39)
7 large prairie point leaves (page 50)
4 small prairie point leaves (page 50)

Supplies
6″ length of green ribbon (1″-wide)
    gathered to 2″ long
18″ metallic ribbon (4mm-wide)
4 double-headed green stamens
antique button 1/2″-3/4″ (the one
    shown is Victorian)
small sprig of millinery flowers or artificial baby's breath
beads for fuchsias and dewdrop on rose
3″ x 4″ piece of crinoline
3″ x 4″ piece of felt or Ultrasuede
pin back

Flower Fashioning Notes

❀ Use the stitched gathered rose technique for both parts of the large pink rose. The center is a 12″ length of 1″-wide dark pink ribbon, gathered and stitched to crinoline. The outer petals are a ruffle from a 15″ length of 1″-wide grosgrain ribbon, gathered and overlapped around the center.

❀ For the flat rosebud, use a 3″ length of 1″-wide pink grosgrain ribbon and a 4″ length of 1″-wide green ribbon for the green wrap calyx.

❀ For the small cabochon rose, cut three 2″ lengths from 1″-wide pink/aqua ombre for the three outer petals and one 8″ length of 1/2″-wide pink embroidery silk ribbon for the center (make a small coiled rose or a folded rose tacked flat to the crinoline).

❀ Use the single u-gather to make the fantasy flowers with stamens or bead centers. Cut a 3″ length of 3/8″-wide ribbon and a 4″ length of 1/2″-wide ribbon.

❀ For the three faux fuchsias, use 3½″ lengths of 1″-wide ribbon strung on gold thread for each. Leave about 10″ of thread hanging from each faux fuchsia. You'll use this to stitch them to the collage. Embellish the faux fuchsia stem with seed beads and a few accent beads at the top of the flower.

❀ The design has seven large prairie point leaves made from 1½″-wide ribbon in a range of colors and four smaller leaves made from 1″-wide ribbon.

1. Make all the flowers and leaves, referring to the instructions on the page listed for each and the Flower Fashioning Notes above. Feel free to change any color, add to or delete any flower.

2. Gather the 6″ length of green ribbon to 2″ long, using the u-gather technique. Tuck behind the main rose.

3. Make the accent loops with the 18″ length of 4mm metallic ribbon. Loop the ribbon 4-6 times, mix in the

green stamens, and secure with stitches.

4. Pin all the elements to a 3″ x 4″ piece of crinoline. Making sure the elements overlap, stitch them to the crinoline in the following order:

a. main rose (positioned as shown in the photo)

b. cabochon rose

c. all the large leaves

d. green ruffle

e. millinery flowers, small filler flowers, and flat bud

f. button and small leaves to fill holes

g. dewdrop bead (on main rose)

h. faux fuchsias (use the hanging threads)

5. Be sure the crinoline doesn't show through and stitch any flower that seems loose or wants to pop up.

6. Trim the excess crinoline around the edges of the collage. Cut a piece of felt or Ultrasuede to fit over the back.

7. Stitch a pin back to this and stitch or glue the backing over the crinoline.

Detail of brooch with roses and faux fuchsias.

Ribbon Flowers in a Garden Urn

Roses and an assortment of other fabulous ribbon flowers fill the urn on this magnificent hall table.

What could be more spectacular than a vase of flowers on a stand in the hallway of your home? Make several stems of your favorite ribbon flowers or use the suggested flowers below to create the arrangement in the photo.

The overall height of the entire arrangement is 24″. The small black cast iron garden urn measures 9½″ tall.

YOU WILL NEED:

Ribbon Flowers & Buds
5 stems of delphinium (page 42)
4 blended tea roses and 3 rosebuds
  (page 64)
5 carnations (page 44)
5 poppies and 4 buds (page 28)
3 stems of sweet peas (page 26)

Purchased Greenery
3 stems of eucalyptus
2 stems of ficus leaves
5 stems of variegated buttonleaf
4 stems of maidenhair fern
2 stems of English ivy

Supplies
small garden urn
Styrofoam ball to snugly fit container

Flower Fashioning Notes

❀ I chose to make cream-colored blended tea roses (shown on page 64). Make the buds with a folded rose center and four rolled corner petals.
❀ Make the carnations with 40″ lengths of 1½″-wide ribbon.
❀ Stem each flower with 18″ of 18-gauge wire and wrap the stems with floral tape. Trim the stems to the right height when you place each flower in the composition.

1. Make all the flowers and buds, referring to the instructions on the page listed for each and the Flower Fashioning Notes above.

2. Position the Styrofoam ball securely near the top of the urn and glue if necessary.
3. Arrange the flowers and greenery in a fanned peacock tail shape. Start at the top and sides and work down in the following order:
a. eucalyptus at the sides and center
b. delphiniums across the top
c. fill in with some buttonleaf stems
d. add a few carnations and rosebuds below the delphiniums
e. add the tea roses about halfway down
f. mix in a few poppies
g. add some ficus leaves, more buttonleaf, a little maidenhair fern, and a few poppy buds
h. add more carnations and poppies
i. fill in the bottom with sweet peas, English ivy, and ferns
4. Cut up small pieces of greenery and fill in any obvious gaps.

Framed P...
Bouquet

Ribbonwork is shown to advantage when mounted on acid-free velvet matte board and set in a deep shadow box.

A bouquet of flowers is always a thoughtful gift. Make a charming bouquet of pansies, bl... bells, and apple blossoms and have them framed in a shadow box. Try other combinatio... of flowers ~ roses, Canterbury bells, and sweet peas make a lovely bridesmaid's posy.

YOU WILL NEED:

Ribbon Flowers & Leaves
2 stemmed pansies (page 22)
1 stem of apple blossoms (page 31)
1 stem of bluebells (page 34)
3 stems of prairie point leaves (page 50)
7-8 stem tubes (page 20)

Supplies
shadow box or frame
1/2 yd. organdy ribbon to tie around
    stems (1″-wide)
optional: sprig of vintage millinery
    greenery, velvet berries, or other
    treasure

Flower Fashioning Notes

❁ Make the two stemmed pansies from 1″-wide blue ombre and pink to mint green ombre ribbons. Add yellow stamen centers. Wrap the stems with floral tape and cover with silk stem tubes.

❁ Make four apple blossoms on a stem, using a continuous 4-petal u-gather from silk embroidery ribbon 1/2″ wide x 6″ long. Each center has one green stamen and four yellow stamens. Stem each blossom with thin wire and wrap with floral tape. Make a cluster of blossoms by wrapping all the stems together.

❁ For the stem of bluebells, use blue ombre ribbon 1″ wide x 2½″ long for each bell. Add a green stamen center and wrap together with floral tape.

❁ Make the three stems of prairie point leaves using olive green ombre ribbon 1″ wide x 2½″ long for each leaf. Make three leaves per stem and wrap each stem with floral tape.

❁ Make the stem tubes from green bias cut silk ribbon 1″ wide x 6″ long for each tube. Wrap each stem with floral tape. Slip stem tubes over the pansy stems.

1. Make all the flowers and leaves, referring to the instructions on the page listed for each and the Flower Fashioning Notes.

2. Arrange the posy. Stitch the leftover floppy stem tubes together at the top and position them within the posy arrangement.

3. Secure all the stems and tubes together with a piece of wire (discarded ribbon wire will do) and cover with enough organdy ribbon to hide the wire.

4. Tie a nice full bow with the organdy ribbon.

5. Mount in a shadow box or frame of your choice.

Victorian Waxed Roses on a Box

Using a favorite Victorian technique for preserving real flowers, the ribbon roses on this box have been dipped in hot wax. Left to cool and harden, they can be used in posies. When back-lit with sunlight, the waxed flowers take on a golden hue. However, it is best if you treat waxed ribbon flowers as you would candles by not leaving them in direct sun.

At a quick glance you may see an autumn-toned posy of wild roses and berries gracing the top of a box. But take a closer look at the roses in the posy. The ribbon has a different look than usual. The flowers have been dipped in wax! The Victorians loved this age-old technique for preserving real flowers, so why not try it on ribbon flowers? Make this posy and set it atop a box, frame it, or simply set it on a shelf.

YOU WILL NEED:

Ribbon Flowers
2 wild roses with stamens (page 61)
1 folded rose (page 59)

Purchased Greenery
stem of autumn-colored millinery
    berries with leaves
cream-colored paper ivy stem
pkg. silk maple leaves in tan/gold/burnt
    orange

Supplies
4″ x 6½″ papier mâché box
22-gauge wire
2 yds. sheer gold ribbon (3″-wide)
box of household paraffin wax (used
    for canning and candle making)

1. Because the color of the ribbon will change when waxed, test your ribbons before making the flowers. Follow the manufacturer's directions and melt wax in a small double boiler. Use tongs to dip a 2″ test piece of each ribbon in melted wax. The color will change to a deeper tone.
2. After you've tested the ribbons and chosen the ones you like, make the flowers, referring to the instructions on the page listed for each. I strongly recommend making a few extra flowers in case something doesn't go quite to your liking.
3. Heat the wax and dip a few practice flowers until you feel proficient. Hold the flower by the stem and insert it upside-down into the melted wax, much like dipping a caramel apple. Cover the entire flower, lift it out of the wax, and let the wax drip off.

4. Place the dipped flower in a vase or other container to cool, making sure it doesn't touch any other surface. Handle with care ~ waxed flowers are easily damaged if bumped.
5. When all the flowers have cooled, carefully wrap the stems with perle cotton or bias ribbon and arrange the berries and leaves with the roses as desired.

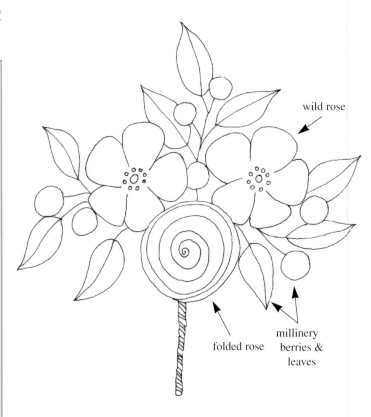

wild rose

folded rose

millinery berries & leaves

6. Wire all the pieces together and wrap the combined stems with more perle cotton or bias ribbon.
7. Tie a sheer gold bow around the stem, leaving the tails long. Gently set the posy aside.
8. Glue a piece of the paper ivy around the outside bottom of the unfinished papier mâché box. Add a few maple leaves for color and cover the whole outside with a length of sheer gold ribbon. Glue the raw edges inconspicuously.
9. Glue a few ivy and maple leaves to the lid.
10. For a fancy addition, I glued a crocheted doily on the lid before gluing on the flower posy.

Woodland Nest

The Canterbury Bell Fairy has found a dear little mouse asleep inside this woodland nest.

Cicely Mary Barker's Flower Fairy™ illustrations have always been a favorite of mine, so I couldn't resist including a fairy in one of my ribbon designs. The Canterbury Bell Fairy was the inspiration for creating this charming woodland scene. Do you see the little dormouse asleep in his nest?

Use this arrangement as a table centerpiece for a baby shower or other special event or display it on a shelf with one or two volumes of the Flower Fairy books.

YOU WILL NEED:

Ribbon Flowers & Leaves
3 stems of Canterbury bells (page 32)
3 stems of prairie point leaves (page 50)

Supplies
nest bundle
Canterbury Bell Flower Fairy
carved wooden mouse
moss
1 yd. green/lavender crossweave ribbon
   (2″-wide) for bow

Flower Fashioning Note

❀ Make 15 prairie point leaves from pieces of ribbon 1″ wide x 2½″ long. Make three stems, with five leaves per stem.

1. Make all the flowers and leaves, referring to the instructions on the page listed for each and the Flower Fashioning Note above.
2. Cut away some of the twigs at the front of the nest bundle and place a small amount of moss in the nest. Lay the mouse on top of the moss.
3. Arrange the leaves in the back and at the sides. Position the Canterbury bells on the sides and toward the front.
4. Tie the ribbon around the nest bundle and finish with a bow.
5. Glue one of the fairy's feet to the bow and one hand to a twig.

Cabochon Rose Lampshade

Small sprays of cabochon roses were very popular ribbonwork decorations during the first part of this century and in particular the 1920s. This new interpretation adorns a vintage English lampshade.

Small lamps with fabric lampshades are easily trimmed with charming cabochon roses. Drawing on inspiration from the roses on the 1920's dress, you too can easily make a crinoline-based rose spray for any decorative use. Stitch them onto a blouse, dressing gown, purse, or cushion.

YOU WILL NEED:

Ribbon Flowers & Leaves
1 cabochon rose (page 66)
1 cabochon bud (page 67)
3 purple filler flowers (page 30)
8 mitered leaves (page 52)

Supplies
chenille needle #22
32-gauge wire
#5 perle cotton or heavy silk thread in
    green to match leaves
8″ x 4″ piece of crinoline
4mm pale blue silk embroidery ribbon
4mm yellow silk embroidery ribbon

Flower Fashioning Notes

✣ For the cabochon rose and cabochon bud, make four petals from pink ombre ribbon 1½″-wide x 2½″ long. Keep one for the bud.

✣ For the rose center, cut a 10″ length of 1/2″-wide (13mm) pink silk embroidery ribbon. Cut a 2″ length of the same pink ribbon for the bud center and a 2″ length of green silk embroidery ribbon 1/2″-wide (13mm) for the bud calyx.

✣ Stitch the forget-me-nots with French knots of blue 4mm silk embroidery ribbon.

✣ Make the three purple filler flowers using 3″ lengths of 1/4″-wide purple ribbon for each. Add yellow knots for the centers, made from 4mm yellow silk embroidery ribbon.

✣ Make eight mitered leaves using 3½″ lengths of 1″-wide green ombre ribbon for each leaf.

✣ For the stems, cut three 7″ lengths of 32-gauge wire for each stem and wrap each with green perle cotton or heavy silk thread. (Refer to page 20.)

1. Make all the flowers and leaves, referring to the instructions on the page listed for each and the Flower Fashioning Notes.

2. Stitch the wrapped stems to the crinoline, using the photo as a guide. Stitch the leaves on top of the stems and then the flowers in the following order:
a. cabochon rose
b. bud
c. three sprays of forget-me-nots (one along each curved stem)
d. three filler flowers

3. Carefully trim the excess crinoline with sharp pointed scissors and stitch the crinoline to your project.

Edwina is enjoying the outdoors under this arbor covered in roses, hollyhocks, and delphiniums.

Several things inspired this project ~ a love of garden architecture and furniture, hats, and teddy bears. I don't have an arbor, but I do have a lovely garden seat, lots of hats, and two bears of whom I am rather fond.

Constance is the larger of the two bears and looks quite endearing. She is dressed in an old-looking pinafore. Edwina is the smaller bear, with a sweet face and a pointed nose. She is naked. Or was, but not any more. I thought she'd look grand in an Edwardian driving hat and a coat. So here she is, sitting on a garden bench just charming the wings right off the bees! (Do you see the bee?)

If you have bears or dolls you would like to show off in a pretty setting, this flower-covered arbor is for you.

Most of the supplies are readily available at the local craft shop and the ribbon flowers are easy to fashion ~ simply read all the instructions before you begin.

YOU WILL NEED:

Ribbon Flowers
3 stems of delphiniums (page 42)
5 stems of hollyhocks (page 36)
10 folded mini roses (page 59)

Purchased Greenery
silk ivy
2-3 sprigs of assorted small greenery
18″ piece of green paper ivy

Supplies
7″-8″ bear or doll
vine arbor
vine fairy chair or love seat to fit in the
    opening of the arbor

Flower Fashioning Notes

❋ Make the hollyhocks with pinks, mauves, peach, and claret ombre ribbons.
❋ Each of the ten folded mini roses is made with an 8″ length of 1″-wide yellow/orange ombre ribbon.
❋ Stem all the flowers and wrap the stems with floral tape.

1. Make all the flowers, referring to the instructions on the page listed for each and the Flower Fashioning Notes above.
2. Glue or wire the fairy chair in the arbor.
3. Drape the silk and paper ivy over the top of the arbor and part way down each side. Add some of the smaller pieces of greenery and ivy at the base of each side of the arbor.
4. Arrange the hollyhocks on the right side and the delphiniums on the left side of the arbor. Secure with fine wires hidden behind greenery.
5. Glue or wire the roses to the top left of the arbor.

Topiary of Ivy and Roses

The art of cutting garden shrubs and bushes into interesting shapes ~ especially birds and animals ~ is called topiary. As you can see, this model is not in the shape of an animal or a bird, but a simple round ball.

With their rather formal appearance, topiaries make very nice dining table decorations for special occasions or charming accents on a sideboard or hall table. Topiaries can be of any height. The finished height of this one is 19″. For a whimsical touch, I couldn't resist adding the Flower Fairy!

A classic topiary made up of roses, ivy, and assorted mini flowers. The fairy holds a small ribbon violet.

YOU WILL NEED:

Ribbon Flowers
32 small folded roses (page 59)
10 purple violets (page 24)
5 fantasy flowers (page 30)

Purchased Greenery
1 stem silk or paper hydrangeas in pale
   lavender/blue (Separate the florets
   and glue singly to the topiary. You
   will not use the entire stem.)
several small stems of silk and paper
   ivy in green
small pieces of greenery

Supplies
metal pot 4½″ tall x 6″ diameter (For
   an informal look, try a clay pot.)
16″ twig approx. 3/4″ in diameter (You
   can use a dowel, but you'll need to
   paint or cover it with ribbon.)
plaster of paris
Styrofoam disk (6″ round x 1½″ deep)
   to fit snugly inside pot
Styrofoam ball (6″ diameter)
moss
16″ square of green fabric
Flower Fairy with wire pick (I used the
   Wayfaring Tree Fairy.)
1 yd. sheer green ribbon for bow (2″-
   wide)
30 pieces green bias cut silk ribbon
   7/16″ and 5/8″ wide x 7″ long tied
   in bows, shoelace style (Use different
   greens and tie different size bows.)
hot glue gun and glue sticks

Flower Fashioning Notes

❋ Make some of the 32 small folded roses with 1″ wide x 8″ long ribbon and others with 1″ wide x 12″ long ribbon. Make four of each color ~ sheer pink, pale pink, pink, rose, peach, yellow, claret, and red. Small

gathered roses also work using the same measurements.
❋ Make three of the ten purple violets with stamens, and seven with beads or French knot centers. Stem and wrap one violet for the fairy to hold.
❋ Use the single u-gather technique to make the five fantasy flowers from 1/2″ wide x 4″ long and 3/4″ wide x 5″ long ribbon in an assortment of lavender and purple, wired and unwired.

1. Make all the flowers, referring to the instructions on the page listed for each and the Flower Fashioning Notes above.
2. Cover the Styrofoam ball with green fabric. Draw the raw fabric edges together on the underside of the ball and glue.
3. Cut the top of the twig at an angle or point. Dab glue on the upper 3″ and push the twig into the ball (about 3½″), pushing in any raw fabric edges.
4. Place the 1½″ Styrofoam disk on the bottom of the twig and push it up about 6″.
5. Follow the manufacturer's directions for mixing plaster. Fill the pot 2/3 full of plaster to weight down the pot and secure the twig.
6. Set the twig in the pot so it touches the bottom. Slide down the foam disk until it just sits in the wet plaster. About 8″ of the twig will show between the rim of the pot and the underside of the covered ball. Let the plaster set until hard (about two hours).
7. Use pins to mark quarter divisions in the ball (this will help with flower and leaf placement).
8. Glue the components to the green fabric in the following order:
   a. paper ivy leaves
   b. silk ivy leaves
   c. variety of roses on each quarter
   d. more silk ivy and paper hydrangea florets
   e. violets, filler flowers, more ivy
   f. silk ribbon bows
9. Glue moss to the top of the pot, so it covers all the Styrofoam.
10. Glue a violet in the Flower Fairy's hand. Insert a wire into the fairy and set her into the moss and Styrofoam.
11. Tie the sheer ribbon around the pot and finish with a bow.

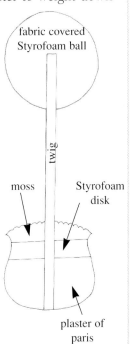

fabric covered Styrofoam ball

twig

moss

Styrofoam disk

plaster of paris

Miniature Rose Bouquet for a Crystal Vanity Box

Set among antique jars, a silver brush, hand mirror, and exquisite lace, the dressing table is a perfect place to showcase your ribbonwork. The crystal box is adorned with a miniature rose posy in taupe and pink ribbons.

A lady's dressing table of the 1920s offered many opportunities to showcase ribbonwork ~ decorated powder puffs, mirrors, pin holders, handkerchief sachets, and boxes are just a few of the items you might have seen.

Showcase your ribbonwork on lovely crystal boxes and pots and display them on your dresser. The small bouquet of miniature blended roses, millinery trims, and stamens shown in the photo is very elegant in its palette of taupe, grey, and pink. By putting a pin back on the composition, you could wear the flowers as a corsage. Adapt some of the same elements to fit a smaller crystal box and a petite picture frame.

This is a perfect project for all those bits and pieces you've been collecting. Look in your box of old trims for some treasures to use to embellish the box.

YOU WILL NEED:

Ribbon Flowers
3 blended roses (page 64)
2 small dark taupe folded roses
(page 59)

Purchased Greenery
3 3″ stems of old millinery lily of the valley or artificial baby's breath
small 3-leaf spray of millinery leaves in taupe silk and velvet
3/4″ velvet millinery pod with leaves

Supplies
4″ round cut crystal box with lid
4″ wide ribbon or 4″ circle of silk or velvet fabric to cover lid
12″ of pink/taupe bias cut ribbon for bow (7/16″-wide)
3 jeweled stamens
12 mixed vintage stamens (vary the shape and color)

Left: Miniature tea roses, folded roses, and millinery trims combine for an elegant posy. The posy could also be worn as a brooch.

Flower Fashioning Notes

❈ Make the three blended roses with a folded rose center and five rolled corner petals. Add three jeweled stamens inside the folded center of one rose. All the folded centers should be 7″ long. Make two of the folded centers with 3/4″-wide variegated embroidery ribbon and the third with 1″-wide grosgrain ribbon. The outer rolled corner petals are from 1″-wide grosgrain or 1⅜″ (32mm) wide x 2½″ long silk embroidery ribbon.

❈ Make the two small dark taupe folded roses from 4″ lengths of 1/2″ (13mm) or 3/4″ (18mm) wide silk embroidery ribbon.

1. Make all the flowers, referring to the instructions on the page listed for each and the Flower Fashioning Notes above.
2. Cover the lid of the crystal box with ribbon or fabric and secure it with glue at the edges.
3. Tie a bow in the pink/taupe bias cut ribbon.
4. Stem the roses by gluing a 2″ piece of 32-gauge wire into the base of each. Cover all the raw edges and stems with taupe perle cotton. The wired stems help the flowers to sit up. For a slightly flatter look, eliminate this step and stitch all the elements to crinoline. Bunch the stamens. These are used as buds in this composition.
5. Arrange all the pieces as shown in the photo, securing with stitches to the crinoline or by wiring the stems together.
6. Stitch or glue the posy to the covered lid.

Wildwood Brooch

*T*he summer is spent and all that remains are the last of the wild roses, some early berries, a few flowers, and the first flush of fallen leaves. Add to this scene some lace and beadwork and you have the makings for a fantastic ribbon collage. The components have been selected to capture the mood of days gone by and those of yesteryear. If not wearing the brooch, it would be very pretty in a richly carved or very ornate frame.

A vintage needlecraft magazine, Victorian needles, old ribbons, lace, and buttons lend inspiration for this collage brooch of leaves, small flowers, lace, a wild rose, and beads.

YOU WILL NEED:

Ribbon Flowers & Leaves

1 faux wild rose (page 61)
1 marigold (see Delphinium, page 42)
1 mini gathered rose (page 57)
1 fantasy flower (page 30)
4 small berries (page 35)
7 large prairie point leaves (page 50)
4 small prairie point leaves (page 50)

Supplies

6″ length of tan ribbon (3/4″-wide) for the filler ruffle
4″ x 2″ piece of old fine lace
assortment of beads (drops, facets, extra large bugles, seed beads)
3″ x 3″ piece of crinoline
3″ x 3″ piece of wool felt or Ultrasuede (to cover the crinoline when the brooch is complete)
large pin back

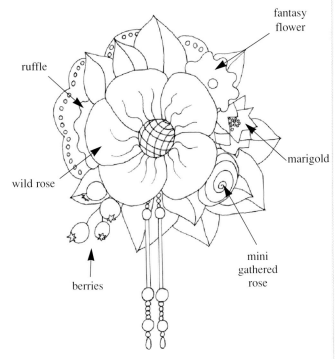

Flower Fashioning Notes

❀ For the wild rose, cut five 4½″ lengths from 1½″-wide burgundy ribbon and make five single u-gather petals. For a smaller flower, use 3″ lengths of 1″-wide ribbon for the petals. Cover the center with unraveled metallic cord for the stamens and cover that with a vintage button. Shape the petals so they cup out.

❀ For the faux marigold, cut four 1″ lengths from 1″-wide gold bias cut silk ribbon and make like the delphinium floret (page 42) except substitute stamens with small pieces of yellow thread bunched together. Use all four ribbon pieces for one flower. Stitch through all the layers to secure.

❀ For the mini gathered rose, use a 6″ length of 1″-wide plum ribbon.

❀ For the fantasy flower, use a 4″ length of 1/2″-wide sheer ribbon with gold metallic edging.

❀ For the berries, use a 2″ length of 3/4″-wide ribbon per berry in purple, plum, and blue.

❀ Use a variety of colors when making the large and small prairie point leaves.

1. Make all the flowers and leaves, referring to the instructions on the page listed for each and the Flower Fashioning Notes. Even though all the flowers and leaves may not show in the photo, make everything listed. You'll have a sufficient number of pieces to create your own design, so don't feel obligated to copy this one. The instructions below are just guidelines.

2. Gather the 6″ length of tan ribbon to 1″ long.

3. Pin all the components in place before stitching. Stitch to the crinoline in the following order, overlapping all the pieces:

a. wild rose
b. lace (behind rose, near top and left)
c. large leaves (top, right, and bottom of rose)
d. mini gathered rose, fantasy flower, and marigold (right of rose)
e. small leaves
f. ribbon ruffle (left of rose)
g. berries (bottom left)

4. Make the bead dangles with the beads in the following order: seed, round facet, long bugle, round facet, seed, round facet, seed, drop bead. With a long single thread, start at the top of one dangle, go down through all the beads then back through until you are at the top again. When you place the dangle in the design, secure both threads by stitching them through the crinoline several times. Cut the thread and glue the knot. Repeat for as many dangles as desired.

5. Clip away excess crinoline in the back. Cut a piece of felt or Ultrasuede to fit over the back.

6. Stitch a pin back to the felt or Ultrasuede and stitch or glue the backing over the crinoline.

*Classic
Rose
Cushion*

When I saw this fabulous burgundy fabric with its embossed leaf pattern, I knew it would be perfect for the cushion I had in mind. The long gold fringing, rich burgundy roses, and masses of leaves help to give it that wonderful classic look so suited to a library or den. Consider making a set of matching curtain tiebacks incorporating the same fabric, roses, and trim.

The three main roses are all different blended tea roses, using a variety of ribbons and techniques. No two are alike ~ one is a full blown rose with sheer petals (see the Petal Guide that follows) around the stamens; the second is a full blown rose with solid burgundy petals around the stamens; the third is shown in 3/4 view.

You can make all three roses like the one in the Petal Guide, however I encourage you to use variety in your composition by adapting two of the roses. Use the techniques you learned in Chapter 4. Create! Experiment! The blended roses on page 64 would be perfect to adapt.

Flower Fashioning Notes

❀ To make the rosebuds, spent roses, and three blended roses you'll need:
a. 7 yds. burgundy ribbon (1½″-wide)
b. 1 yd. gold ribbon (1½″-wide)

c. 1½ yds. brown/raspberry ombre ribbon (1″-wide)
d. 1½ yds. brown/raspberry ombre ribbon (1½″-wide)
e. 1 yd. sheer burgundy ribbon (1½″-wide)
❀ Make the three large blended roses using the Petal Guide below or adapt the second and third roses from other blended tea roses. Alter as desired.
Alternative: Make the third rose a 3/4 view (shown) with a continuous 4-petal u-gather (1″ wide x 8½″ long) around the stamens followed by eight rolled corner petals (1½″ wide x 3½″ long). Three petals are in the second row with the remaining five petals stitched on one side only.

Petal Guide
Row 1: 1 sheer continuous 3-petal u-gather x 9½″ long, tightly secured around stamens
Row 2: 5 burgundy rolled corner petals x 3½″ long
Row 3: 1 sheer u-gather petal x 6″ long
Row 4: 5 burgundy rolled corner petals x 4″ long
Row 5: 1 sheer u-gather petal x 8″ long
Row 6: 5 burgundy rolled corner petals x 4½″ long
Row 7: 1 gold rolled corner petal x 4½″ and 1 gold u-gather petal x 6″ long

❀ Make the three rosebuds from 1½″-wide brown/raspberry ombre using either a folded rose or gathered rose center followed by four rolled corner petals. Cut 10″ for each center and 3½″ for each of the rolled corner petals (three burgundy and one ombre per rosebud). The rosebuds have no stamens, only gathered or folded rose centers.
❀ Make the four spent roses and the falling petal from 1″-wide brown/raspberry ombre ribbon. Cut and make five rolled corner petals x 2½″ long. Two of the spent

---

YOU WILL NEED:

Ribbon Flowers & Leaves
3 large blended roses (page 64 and refer to the Petal Guide)
3 rosebuds (refer to Flower Fashioning Notes)
4 spent roses and 1 falling petal (refer to Flower Fashioning Notes)
17 mitered leaves (page 52)

Purchased Greenery
spray of 3 large millinery leaves in taupe/gold

Supplies
18″ square cushion
15-25 double-headed stamens in olive green/gold for each large rose
4 large double-headed gold stamens for each spent rose
5 small double-headed olive green stamens for each spent rose
22-gauge wire
12″ square of black crinoline

roses will have one petal around the stamens. One of the spent roses will have two petals, and the last spent rose will have no petals, just stamens. Keep the extra petal for the fallen petal.

❋ Make eight mitered leaves from 1½″-wide olive green ribbon and nine mitered leaves from 1½″-wide burgundy/green crossweave ribbon. Cut each leaf 4½″ long.

❋ Stem the buds and spent roses with 3″-5″ pieces of 22-gauge wire and wrap with 5/8″-wide green bias cut silk ribbon. The three large roses have twisted ribbon stems made from olive green ribbon 1½″ wide x 8″ long.

1. Make all the flowers and leaves, referring to the instructions on the page listed for each and the Flower Fashioning Notes.

2. Stitch all the elements to the crinoline in the following order (remember to overlap all the elements when stitching them):

a. large roses in the center
b. tuck in millinery leaves
c. twisted stems below large roses
d. buds and spent roses
e. mitered leaves around the roses as desired

3. You may need to stitch in several places to be completely secure. When finished stitching, trim the excess crinoline from the back of the composition and stitch the crinoline to the cushion.

4. Stitch the fallen leaf to a small piece of crinoline. Trim away the excess and stitch the crinoline to the cushion.

Burgundy tea roses, rich fabric, and elegant gold fringing make this classic cushion a must for any library or den. The roses are made from a variety of ribbons and techniques.

Victorian Purse Necklace

The beautiful jacquard ribbon in this necklace purse is a reproduction of an old French ribbon. The purse is just big enough for a lipstick and a few coins.

Having looked at or made the large vintage handbag on page 98, you might want to try your hand at a small one. A project this size is perfect for small lengths of ribbon, especially the exquisite woven jacquards. The beadwork necklace and fringe really personify the romantic Victorian look.

YOU WILL NEED:

Ribbon Flowers & Leaves

1 miniature folded rose (page 59)

2 miniature boat leaves or leaf loops (page 51)

Supplies

2″ gold tone purse frame

7½″ length of jacquard ribbon (1¾″-wide)

3½″ x 7½″ piece of velvet

3½″ x 7½″ piece of lining fabric

4 pink stamens to use as buds

beads: seed beads, bugle beads, facets, daggers (or substitute the bead necklace with a narrow ribbon or chain)

jewelry findings: 2 clamshells

1″ square of crinoline

metallic gold thread to stitch purse to frame

glue to secure beading knots

trim for inside purse lining

Flower Fashioning Notes

❁ Make the miniature folded rose from a 3″ length of 3/8″-wide ruffle-edged ribbon.

❁ Make the two miniature boat leaves or loops from a 1½″ length of 3/16″-wide green ribbon per leaf/loop.

1. Make the flower and leaves/loops, referring to the instructions on the page listed for each and the Flower Fashioning Notes above. This is tricky and fiddly because of the small size.

2. Bunch the stamen heads in a cluster.

3. Stitch all the elements to crinoline. Trim the excess crinoline and set aside.

4. Cut out the pattern twice, once from velvet and once from lining fabric. Center the jacquard ribbon vertically on the piece of velvet. Pin, then stitch it in place with hidden slip stitches. Trim the ribbon piece to match the shape of the velvet on the curved ends.

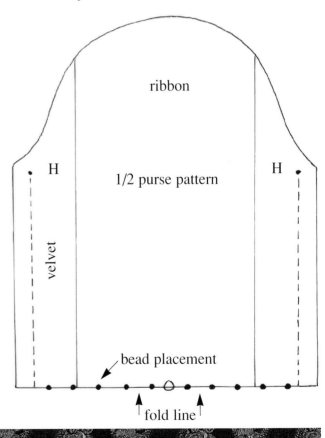

ribbon

H   1/2 purse pattern   H

velvet

bead placement

fold line

5. Baste across the bottom of the purse (along the fold) with white thread. This forms a removable guideline for the bead fringe. Apply Fray Check to all the raw edges and set aside.

6. Arrange the beads for the fringe. *Hint:* Set the beads on a piece of felt to keep them from rolling.

7. Using the pattern guide, mark the position of each dangle with a pin along the basted guideline.

8. Thread a milliner's or beading needle with three yards of single white beading thread and triple knot the end. Start with the fancy dangle in the center of the velvet. Secure the knot with glue and bring the thread through to the right side of the velvet. Thread on the bead that is closest to the velvet, followed by each of the beads in the sequence. Return your thread back through all the beads in that dangle and go through the velvet at a point close to the beginning hole. Adjust the tension of the dangle. Using the same thread, bead all the dangles on the right, adjust the tension, and tie off with a triple knot secured with glue. Do not cut the thread. Bead the left side in the same manner as the right. Secure with glue and cut the thread.

9. With right sides together, backstitch up the side seams of the velvet as far as the letter H on the pattern. Turn the purse right side out so the beads are on the outside. Position the velvet so it sits inside the purse frame and the hinge is level with the top of the side seam (the velvet will protrude over the top but you will cut this away after the velvet is stitched to the frame). *Hint:* Hold the velvet in place with two or three temporary stitches. Ease in any fullness across the top as you stitch.

10. Using gold thread, backstitch the velvet to one side of the frame, easing in the fullness as you go. Secure the knots with a dot of glue and cut the thread. Backstitch the rest of the velvet to the other side of the frame and remove the holding stitches.

11. Trim away excess velvet at the top and apply Fray Check to the raw edge.

12. Stitch the crinoline piece with the ribbon rose and leaf decoration to the front of the purse.

13. Stitch the side seams of the lining. Position the lining to fit inside the purse. It should be slightly shorter in depth than the purse. Turn the top edge under and glue or slipstitch it to the velvet.

14. Glue the narrow trim over any raw edges or stitches on the lining.

15. To make the necklace, arrange the beads in a pleasing order. Use beading thread doubled to 35″ long. Triple knot the thread around a seed bead and thread it onto a clamshell finding (this hides the knots when closed). Glue the knots to secure. Close the clamshell ball and attach it to the loop on the purse frame. Thread on all the beads to a length of 27″ and then take the thread through the second clamshell. Triple knot around a seed bead and dot with glue. Cut the thread, close the clamshell, and attach it to the other loop on the purse frame.

Wedding Rose Purse

The Wedding Rose is named for its creamy beauty, billowing petals, and sparkling center. Several of these would be fabulous on a wedding gown.

Adorn a simple fabric purse with this beautiful blended ribbon rose which I have named the "Wedding Rose." Use it on a bridal headpiece or as the center decoration on the back of a wedding dress. A cluster of three roses and ivy would be the crowning glory on a wedding cake.

Three styles of ribbon (stripes, solids, sheers), jeweled stamens, and three petal techniques (rolled corner petals, single, and continuous u-gather petals) make this a truly fabulous rose.

YOU WILL NEED:

Ribbon Flowers
1 blended rose (refer to instructions below)
Purchased Greenery
velvet millinery leaf spray
Supplies
7″ x 8″ fabric purse (purchased or handmade)

Flower Fashioning Notes

❋ The wedding rose has 11 jewel, pearl, or metallic gold stamens. You will need cream ribbons in the following styles and widths to create a 5″ diameter rose:
1 yd. sheer (2″-wide)
1 yd. fancy striped ribbon (1½″-wide)
1/2 yd. solid (1″-wide)
1/2 yd solid (1½″-wide)
2 yds. solid (2″-wide)

❋ Make all the petals using the measurements in parenthesis below for *each petal*. Keep each row of petals separate. Follow the Petal Guide below. Begin the rose with the stamens stitched together in a bunch, then stitch the first row of petals around the stamen center. All other rows are stitched on clockwise. Each petal should be evenly spaced.

Petal Guide
Row 1: inner petals ~ one continuous 4-petal u-gather (8¼″ length of 1″-wide solid ribbon)
Row 2: 3 single u-gather petals (4″ lengths of 1½″-wide solid ribbon)
Row 3: 2 single u-gather petals (8″ lengths of 2″-wide sheer ribbon)
Row 4: 3 rolled corner petals (4″ lengths of 1½″-wide striped ribbon)
Row 5: 3 petals ~ 1 single u-gather (8″ length of 2″-wide sheer ribbon) and 2 rolled corner petals (4″ lengths of 1½″-wide striped ribbon)
Row 6: 5 rolled corner petals (4″ lengths of 2″-wide solid ribbon)
Row 7: 7 rolled corner petals (4½″ lengths of 2″-wide solid ribbon)

1. Make the rose, referring to the Flower Fashioning Notes and the Petal Guide.
2. Cover the back of the rose with ribbon or Ultrasuede.
3. Stitch the millinery leaves to the rose.
4. Stitch a pin back to the rose, then attach it to the front of the purse.

The two roses below are interpretations of the Wedding Rose done by my students. Neither of them is exactly like the sample and yours won't be either, simply because we are all different people, with different tastes, senses of color, and stitching abilities.

Vicki's

Kimberly's

Yours

Vintage Purse

The ribbonwork on this fabulous velvet purse is made up of just one element ~ leaves! The purse is trimmed with antique metallic lace, a Victorian button, new beads, and new velvet which has been "distressed" to appear old.

I found the vintage metallic lace on the front of this purse while on a trip back to Australia. The leaf pattern on the lace inspired me to design the purse. The velvet used is new and got its "vintage" appearance with some bleach and a little help from me. I call this "distressing" velvet.

Start with a small bowl of bleach and some water (be sure to wear rubber gloves). Toss in the velvet, tightly scrunch it up, and let it sit for awhile. Check it after ten minutes and then periodically until you get the look you like. Rinse the fabric thoroughly, then wash it in the washing machine and tumble dry. Lightly press on the wrong side. Yes, I realize I have committed every sin in caring for velvet, but . . . the result is wonderful. Experiment. I've had rose pink turn to mottled peach; hunter green to fabulous drab olive/brown, etc. Beautiful!

This may be the perfect project for some of those treasures you have stashed away. I encourage you to substitute materials as needed or to choose fabrics and colors that appeal to you and simply use my model as a guide.

YOU WILL NEED:

Ribbon Leaves
25 prairie point leaves (page 50)
4 boat leaves (page 51)

Supplies
5" gold tone purse frame (If you use a different style or size frame, you will need to adjust the shape of the top of the fabric pattern as well as the size of the bag.)
42" chain for shoulder strap (24" chain for a hand held purse)
2 round jump rings (7mm)
18" x 9" piece of velvet, distressed or plain
18" x 9" piece of lining fabric to coordinate with velvet
lace to cover 2/3 front of purse
antique button, buckle, charm, or elegant "do-dad"
beads: seed, bugle, droplet beads for tassels on lace and dewdrops on leaves, seed beads for edging around frame
narrow trim for inside purse to cover lining stitches
buttonhole twist (thread) to match velvet
7" x 4" piece of crinoline

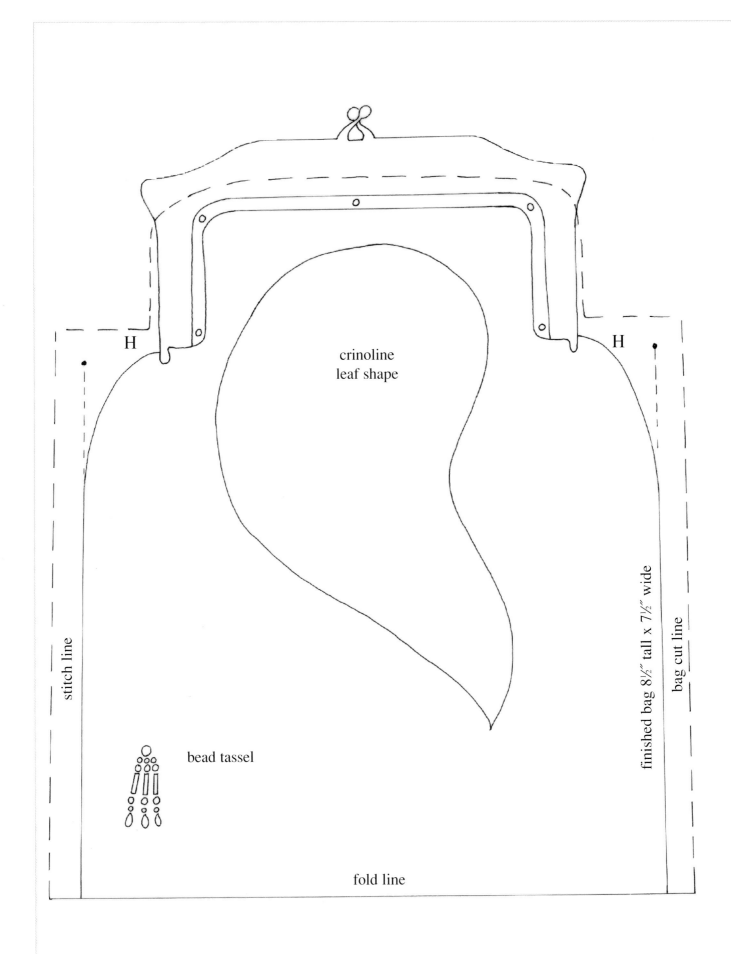

H

H

crinoline
leaf shape

stitch line

finished bag 8½″ tall x 7½″ wide

bag cut line

bead tassel

fold line

Flower Fashioning Note

✿ Make 25 autumn and green-toned prairie point leaves from 1½"-wide ribbon and four boat leaves from 1"-wide ribbon. Remember your "bag o' leaves?" This is the perfect chance to use some of them.

1. Make the leaves, referring to the instructions on the page listed for each and the Flower Fashioning Note.
2. Using a photocopy machine or graph paper, enlarge the pattern to size (9¾" tall x 8¼" wide) and cut one from the velvet and one from the lining fabric. With right sides together, stitch the sides of the lining. Start at the fold and end at the letter H (hinge). Set aside.
3. Stitch the lace to all sides of the velvet and set aside.
4. Cut a piece of crinoline in a leaf shape (from the pattern). Refer to the photo for placement and pin the leaves to the crinoline. Start with the prairie point leaves at the base, then build upward. The boat leaves are most effective on top of the prairie point leaves because they hide the raw edges of the leaf below. When you're satisfied with the arrangement, stitch the leaves in place.
5. Add a few bead "dewdrops" and a fabulous antique button or bead at the top of the arrangement. Trim the excess crinoline from the back and set aside.
6. Make the bead tassels with three dangles to each tassel (refer to the pattern).
7. Using gold or matching thread, stitch each tassel cluster to a point on the lace.
8. Stitch the crinoline with the leaves to the front of the purse about 1" down from the purse frame.
9. With right sides together, sew up the sides of the velvet purse starting at the bottom and stopping at the letter H (hinge). Turn inside out so the leaves/beads are on the outside. Set aside.
10. Thread a needle with buttonhole twist. Position the lining so it sits inside the purse frame and the hinge is level with the top of the side seam. Turn under the raw edges at the top and tack down. Stitch the lining to the inside of one side of the purse frame, using back-stitches while easing in the fullness across the top. When complete, stitch the other side of the lining to the other side of the frame.

11. Position the velvet so it sits outside the purse frame and the hinge is level with the top of the side seam. Turn under the raw edges of the velvet and tack the top edge down. Stitch the velvet fabric to the front of the frame with backstitches, easing in any fullness as you go. Stitch each side of the bag to the frame separately.
12. Cover the stitches around the front side of the purse with a row of seed beads couched to the stitch line. Cover the stitch line on the inside of the frame with a narrow piece of braid or ribbon trim stitched or glued in place. Tuck in any raw edge that might pop out near the hinges and secure with a few stitches if necessary.
13. Attach the chain to the frame with the jump rings.

Millinery catalog, circa 1880.

The Millinery Collection: Hats circa 1870 to the present perch on vintage hat stands. (Collections of Helen Gibb, Janice Page, and Laurie Ramesbothom)

Spring Hat with Fancy Peony

With its extravagant bloom and alluring veiling, this hat could be worn to any number of special occasions including a wedding, a garden party, or to tea at the Brown Palace and Ritz hotels. Even if you do not wear hats, it would make a splendid display in your bedroom if set on an old hat stand or hung from a hall tree in your foyer.

This pink bloom is the ultimate in peony techniques! The difference between this version and the quick peony is the two ribbon colors and widths and the layering of the four petal techniques. Your hat will be beautiful whether you use a quick peony or the fancy peony shown.

YOU WILL NEED:

Ribbon Flowers & Leaves
1 fancy peony (page 46)
5 boat leaves (page 47)

Supplies
wide brimmed white hat
1 yd. of creamy pink bias cut satin silk ribbon (2½″-wide) for the hatband
2 yds. of creamy pink bias cut silk ribbon (5/8″-wide) for the looped streamers
1 yd. of 15″-wide cream colored silk hat veiling for the bow/loop

Flower Fashioning Note

❋ For the peony, I used 55″ of 1½″-wide creamy pink bias cut ribbon, 40″ of 1½″- wide pale pink bias cut ribbon, and 57″ of 2½″-wide pale pink bias cut ribbon.

FASHIONING SECRET

Instead of permanently stitching the peony to the hat, tack a brooch pin to the back of the flower so it is removable.

1. Make the flower and leaves, referring to the instructions on the page listed for each and the Flower Fashioning Note.

2. Mark the front and back of the hat crown with a pin. Leave the pin in place until the hat is completely trimmed.

3. With the hat on your head, position the hatband ribbon around the base of the crown and have someone help you pin it in place. Measure the length of ribbon needed and add 2″ so it will overlap in the back. Make and stitch two pleats at each cut end, just like the pleated petal. Stitch a few tiny stitches at the base of the crown to secure the hatband in the front and at each side. Overlap the pleats on the back of the hatband and stitch at the back of the crown.

4. Make the net "loop" by folding the net in half widthwise. Stitch across its middle, about 10″ from the fold, and gather. Stitch the loop to the back of the hat at an angle.

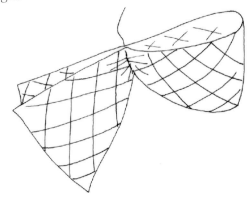

5. Make six silk ribbon loops and stitch them to the center back.

6. Stitch stem wires on the back of the boat leaves and wrap the ends of the leaves and stems with perle cotton. Group three leaves together and stitch them to the right side of the hat under the net bow. Stitch the other two leaves to the left side, on top of the net.

7. Pin the peony in the center of the back or secure with large tacking stitches.

Vintage Summer Hat with Roses

A horsehair driving hat with French roses, circa 1908, was the inspiration for the new straw hat with roses and peacock feathers.

I enjoy looking through my collection of articles and old books on millinery, and am especially intrigued with the descriptions of the trimmings used. One such article from the Delineator, 1899, recommends the use of tulle, "a dainty diaphanous fabric, susceptible of the most artistic arrangement and producing soft billowy effects."

Another article, from the Ladies Home Journal, 1910, describes the types of trims and flowers popular at the time. "The small flowers, such as violets, primroses and hydrangeas, are charming massed over a crown with a soft satin or tulle bow to give a light and airy touch. On the larger hats, roses in all tones, shading from palest pink to deepest cerise, are lovely, as well as pansies, orchids, and tulips . . . used on light colored straws."

My hat collection has also been very inspiring, and in particular the driving hat, circa 1908. This fabulous old hat measures 18″ across, is made of a wire frame and covered with real horsehair braid. It has a net hatband, two white silk French roses with leaves, and a gold buckle.

The stylish summer hat shown here is my adaptation of the driving hat. It is made of straw and sports a bell crown with inward sloping sides, sometimes referred to as a madhatter style. The hat is designed with the trimmings just to the left of the front. There are two roses, a bud, green silk veiling, a milliner's bow, and two side feathers from peacocks that my grandfather raised. An antique hatpin completes the trimming.

YOU WILL NEED:

Ribbon Flowers & Leaves
2 blended roses (page 64)
1 rosebud (refer to Flower Fashioning Notes)
3 prairie point leaves (page 50)

Supplies
straw hat (madhatter style)
28″ length of green bias cut silk ribbon (2½″-wide) for the hatband
12″ x 15″ piece of olive green silk veiling
1½ yds. of olive green ribbon with black stripe (1½″-wide) for the milliner's bow
2 peacock side feathers

Flower Fashioning Notes

❀ These blended roses utilize four rose techniques. You will need four yards of 1½″-wide ombre ribbon (raspberry to yellow), cut and made as follows: two 12″ lengths for the small folded rose centers, ten 4″ lengths for the dipped corner petals, 14 4½″ lengths for the rolled corner petals, one 5″ length for the rolled bud center (like the beginning of the folded rose). For contrast add a sheer petal to each rose and one to the bud. Use 5″ lengths of 1½″-wide sheer ribbon for *each* petal, two magenta, and one yellow/orange ombre. Make three single u-gather petals.

❀ The roses are constructed like blended tea roses except that you substitute the centers and some of the petals. The folded rose is the center. Stitch the five dipped corner petals around it, followed by one sheer u-gather petal. Next come the seven rolled corner petals.

❀ Use green ombre ribbon for the three prairie point leaves.

1. Make the flowers and leaves, referring to the instructions on the page listed for each and the Flower Fashioning Notes above.
2. Mark the front and back of the hat crown with a pin. Leave the pins in place until the hat is completely trimmed. Put a pin in the crown to mark the center front.
3. With the hat on your head, position the hatband ribbon around the base of the crown and have some-

one help you pin it in place. Measure the length of ribbon needed and add 2″ so it will overlap. Make and stitch two pleats at each cut end, just like the pleated petal. Overlap the pleats on the hatband and stitch together near the left front of the crown. Stitch a few tiny stitches at the base of the crown to secure the hatband in several places.

4. Gather the silk veiling across its width, about 4″ from the left end. Stitch it to the base of the crown over the hatband seam. The milliner's bow and roses will sit on top of this.

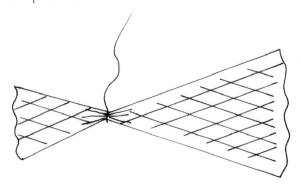

5. Cut a 32½″ length from the striped ribbon for the milliner's bow. The bow is a continuous series of loops in different lengths, gathered and stitched together.

6. Gather across the ribbon as indicated on the diagram below. Secure each gather and match Point 1 to Point 2 and stitch together. This makes the first loop. Repeat for Point 3 and Point 4 and so on until the four loops are made. Stitch the loops together at their base. Set aside.

7. Cut a 12″ length from the striped ribbon for the half rosette. The half rosette is simply a ruffled piece of ribbon using the single u-gather technique. Fan it around the end of the milliner's loops.

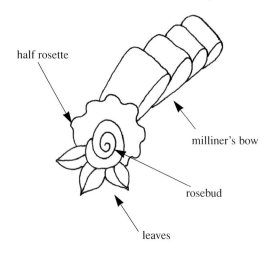

half rosette

milliner's bow

rosebud

leaves

8. Stitch the milliner's bow and the half rosette to the hat.

9. The bud center has a sheer magenta u-gather petal wrapped around it. Stem the bud with 3″ of 20-gauge wire. Wrap the raw edges of the bud and the stem with perle cotton, then stitch the rosebud on top of the rosette so it hides any raw ends of the milliner's bow.

10. Stitch three leaves in front of the bud. Tack the roses to the front of the crown. Add the two peacock feathers and a hatpin.

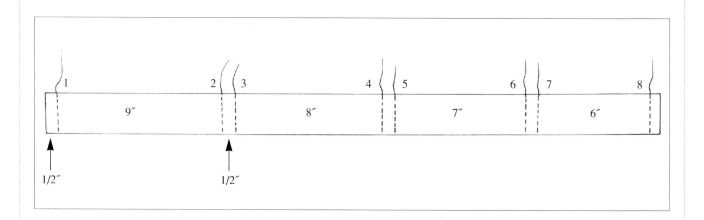

1   2   3   4   5   6   7   8
      9″   8″   7″   6″

1/2″   1/2″

Autumn Hat with Mixed Flowers

A chrysanthemum, folded roses, carnations, and rose hips adorn this felt hat. (Australian hatbox, circa 1935)

When my sister Sue and I were about seven and eight years old, my mother took us to the milliner, Mrs. Edwards, in Enmore, Australia, for custom-made hats. Back then it was considered proper attire for young ladies to wear a hat with their wool suits when out visiting and churchgoing. Sue had a green suit and I had a dark blue one.

When I asked Sue what she remembered about these visits to the milliner she replied, "Oh, the large round fish bowl on the glass counter, of course. I also liked running my fingers over the ball bearings in the glides for the mirrored doors behind the counter!" I wonder what I was doing?

Continuing with the memories, Sue said, "Your hat, Helen, was blue felt with red cherry things all over the crown. Mine was green felt with a covered button at the top. They both had brims that rolled up." I had forgotten all these details! Thank you Sue.

Mum's hat was a pink affair with a diamanté button. It looked a bit like a squashed meringue.

You could wear this brown felt hat with its brim turned up or down. The autumn composition of chrysanthemum, faded roses, rose hips, carnations, and leaves can be placed at the back of the hat, to the side, or over the left front brim. A homemade hatpin of beads makes a lovely finishing touch. If hats are not for you, then arrange these same elements on a piece of crinoline and stitch it to a cushion, tote bag, or have it framed.

A snapshot of the author, her mother, and sister in their hats, about 1959. (Photo courtesy of Sue Barr.)

1. Make the flowers and leaves, referring to the instructions on the page listed for each and the Flower Fashioning Notes.

2. The flower composition is designed for the left front of the hat. Stitch the hatband around the crown, overlapping the tails so the ends sit snugly against the edge of the brim. Remember to fit the hatband while the hat is on your head.

3. It helps to pin everything to the hat first and then make adjustments to the arrangement before you stitch the flowers in place. Begin with the chrysanthemum in the center of the hatband tails. Tuck in the carnations, roses, leaves, and rose hips.

4. Make a hatpin from a hatpin finding. Select unusual beads and secure them to the pin shaft with jewelry glue.

Flower Fashioning Notes

❈ For the chrysanthemum, use 1½ yards each of seven colors (7mm up to 5/8″-wide) bias cut silk ribbon, embroidery silk ribbon, and other narrow ribbons. Select colors *and textures* that blend well (e.g. russet, cinnamon, burgundy, wine, purple, mauve, rose). Cut nine 5½″ lengths of ribbon from each of the seven colors. Keep the colors separate. (You may have leftover ribbon.)

❈ For the ombre folded rose, you'll need 15″ of 1½″-wide raspberry/brown ombre ribbon.

❈ The silk folded rose is made from 15″ of 1½″-wide gold/brown bias cut silk ribbon. Silk ribbon doesn't fold as easily as wired ribbon, so to help shape the petals take a few stitches here and there when stitching the rose to the hat.

❈ You need a 2½″ length of 1″-wide ribbon for each rose hip. Ombres in peach, pink, and wine work well.

❈ To make the two carnations, use an 18″ length of 1″-wide bias cut silk ribbon for each flower. Use cream-colored ribbon with a tinted brown edge.

❈ Make the prairie point leaves from 1½″-wide and 1″-wide ribbons in autumn colors.

❈ Make the three large boat leaves from 1½″-wide ribbon in an assortment of colors.

Winter Hat

The collage brooch makes a stunning decoration on this feather trimmed felt hat. The black velvet cloak, circa 1898 is beautifully embroidered with cut jet. (Cloak courtesy of Emily Gibb)

If the antique hat bug has bitten and you are on the hunt for antique hats with ribbons, you may find fancy well-trimmed hats difficult to locate. One reason is that ladies retrimmed their hats often in order to heed the fashions of the day. After several years of retrimming, many hats simply wore out.

This black felt hat, although not old, has many elements on it that were used in Victorian times. The crown is wrapped in folds of black velvet, while a spray of black feathers perches at a jaunty angle on the back of the turned-up brim. All this black makes the ribbonwork collage brooch really stand out. Although it is simple in design, it is rich in color. Do add a dashing hatpin to complete the hat!

YOU WILL NEED:

Ribbon Flowers & Leaves

4 folded roses (page 59)

10 large prairie point leaves (page 50)

9 small prairie point leaves (page 50)

Supplies

beads: an iridescent bead accent is hidden in the leaves

28″ x 10″ piece of velvet for the hatband

2″ x 3″ piece of black crinoline

12 black 6″ feathers

Flower Fashioning Notes

❀ For the four folded roses use 8″ lengths of 1½″-wide ribbon in a variety of styles and colors.

❀ Note the pink, gold, and lavender prairie point leaves in addition to the many different colored green ones.

1. Make the flowers and leaves, referring to the instructions on the page listed for each and the Flower Fashioning Notes above.
2. Arrange the roses and leaves on a 2″ x 3″ piece of black crinoline, starting with the four roses near the center. Add the leaves around the roses, overlapping big leaves with small ones.
3. Stitch a bead (it will be a bud) on top of the leaves and slightly behind the gold rose.
4. Trim away the excess crinoline and glue or stitch felt or Ultrasuede (stitch a pin back to the felt first) to cover the back.
5. Arrange the black velvet fabric hatband around the crown. Turn under any raw edges and stitch in several places to secure.
6. Stitch the 12 black feathers to a small piece of crinoline in a fan shape, then stitch the fanned feathers to the turned-up brim at the back of the hat. Position the collage brooch over the base of the feathers.

Fashions of the day in cloaks and millinery from the Edward B. Grossman & Company catalog 1898.

Afternoon Tea in the Garden

"*Afternoon tea is an institution entrenched in one's life.*"
Nola Ford, age 69,
Sydney, Australia,
August 1997

Afternoon Tea and Tea Cozy

The tea cozy with ribbon gardenias and a bead tassel lends an elegant touch to this afternoon tea table. Serve dainty sandwiches, scones, and of course, hot tea.

Since tea needs to be kept hot, consider a fancy tea cozy for your teapot as it sits on the tea table. The cozy can be knitted, crocheted, or made from fabric. The one in the photo is made from handkerchief linen with a removable padded liner. Dress it up with some of your ribbonwork flowers such as the gardenia and add a handmade beaded tassel.

There are many tea cozy patterns available in the home decorating section of pattern books at your local fabric shop, but if you're really stuck for a pattern try this: Make a rectangle pattern big enough to fit over your teapot; round the corners (a dinner plate will work), and cut out the fabric for the outer cover. Use quilted fabric for the liner, 1/2″ smaller than the cover. Sew up the liner and then the outer cover. Use a safety pin or velcro to hold them together. Decorate with lace, ribbon flowers, and beads.

Afternoon tea is one of the most enjoyable times of the day. Why not make it a habit to have a cup of tea and a biscuit between three and four o'clock every day? More substantial afternoon teas are lovely for bridge clubs, birthdays, bridal showers, and family gatherings.

Teas can be plain or fancy. I enjoy both. My mother hosts an afternoon tea for me when I travel back to Australia. The relatives gather at our house to enjoy dainty sandwiches, cakes, biscuits, and warm scones. The teapots are filled three or four times!

A menu for a family tea might include small triangle-shaped sandwiches of white or wheat bread with assorted fillings such as curried egg, tomato, cucumber, or cheese with relish. The crusts are always cut off! You might also serve some sausage rolls which are made from finely ground cooked meat, wrapped in puff pastry and baked. The cake might be chocolate with peppermint flavored chocolate icing, an apple tea cake, an orange cake, or a poppyseed cake. Sponge cake, with icing sugar on top and its middle spread with jam and fresh cream is my favorite. The biscuits will vary according to the season, but you could offer chocolate coated ones in the winter and shortbread in the summer. Of course, there are always freshly made scones still warm from the oven. Spread them with raspberry jam and a dollop of cream, and don't bother counting how many you eat!

Black tea is most commonly served for a proper afternoon tea. Some favorites of mine are Twinnings English Breakfast and Blackcurrant and good old Australian Bushells. To make a perfect pot of tea (about six cups), start with boiling water. Rinse out the teapot with some of the boiling water, drop in one tea bag for each person, then fill the teapot with boiling water. Let the tea steep for about five minutes. If you like milk in your tea, pour it in the teacup before the tea. A small teaspoon of sugar is optional.

The tea table can be layered in beautiful lacy tea cloths decorated with small vases of flowers as well as ivy trimmings from the garden. For a bridal tea, swath the edges of the table with tulle and ribbons. And do use your best china! Note the lovely crocheted milk jug cover. It is decorated with beads to give it some weight so it does not blow off the jug. The covers prevent insects from landing in the milk.

My mother tells a tea table story of when she was five years old and her mother was entertaining some bridge friends. "The tea table was set with the best china and all was covered with a cloth until ready to serve. I crawled under the table, and for some unknown reason bumped my head up suddenly and the whole table came crashing to the floor. I was so terrified that I ran away and hid in the linen cupboard. They looked for me for several hours and I remember that it was dark when I was finally discovered. Everyone was so pleased to find me that I didn't get into trouble at all."

Beaded Fuchsias
on a Cream Cushion

Whether using three fuchsias or dozens, they will give your composition movement and life if allowed to dangle.

Cushions are one of the most effective ways to display ribbonwork. This very elegant cream cushion features three delicate fuchsias with beaded stems. It measures 13″ x 9″ and is made from striped silk organza and damask. Use your favorite pattern to make a cushion and simply adapt the fuchsia composition to fit.

For the bride in your family, a silk moiré ring pillow with a cluster of three or five fuchsias in the center caught up with a tiny satin bow to hold the wedding rings, would be exquisite. Or consider a very delicate cushion made of lace with a beaded fuchsia nestled at each corner much like tassels would be used ~ a perfect piece to hold small brooches on your dressing table.

YOU WILL NEED:

Ribbon Flowers
3 beaded frilly fuchsias (page 38)

Supplies
cream-colored cushion (homemade or
    purchased)
3-5 small pearl double-headed stamens
    per flower
1 long fancy or large pearl stamen per
    flower
beads: 3 small bugles, 9 seed beads, 3
    larger pearls, 3 crystal beads

Flower Fashioning Notes

✿ For the upper petals of each flower, use a 5¼″ length of 1½″-wide wired cream grosgrain ribbon.
✿ Make the frill for each flower from a 7″ length of 1½″-wide sheer cream folded in half lengthwise, with both wires removed. Or use a 3/4″-wide single thickness organdy ribbon.

1. Make the fuchsias, referring to the instructions on the page listed and the Flower Fashioning Notes above.
2. Bead each stem with the appropriate number of beads based on the final use for your fuchsias. Leave enough thread to stitch the completed fuchsia to the cushion.

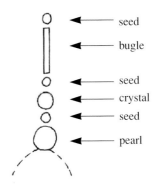

seed
bugle
seed
crystal
seed
pearl

3. Decorate the cushion. Have fun with this part, whether you have only three fuchsias or a hothouse full!

Glossary

Biscuit: cookie

Crossweave: ribbon with the warp thread in one color and the weft in another

Cuppa: cup of tea

Diamante: rhinestone

Fiddly: somewhat awkward

Floret: small flower heads that make up a larger flower

Gathering edge: the side of ribbon that you will gather

Icing sugar: powdered sugar

Ombre: ribbon that gradiates from one shade to another

Perle edge: a fashionable scalloped or picot edging on ribbons during the early 1800s

Plaits: an old-fashioned word for pleats which are a staple in millinery work as well as ribbonwork on clothing

Sarcenet: loosely woven silk, easily draped and used for linings as well as gowns during the early 1800s

Stump: the base of the flower plus the excess that is formed after the ribbon has been folded or rolled up

Tricky: awkward, sometimes leads to frustration so have a cuppa and relax

Wadding: cotton batting

Add some ribbon flowers to a bowl of potpourri and dried flowers for a very unique effect. There are 21 ribbon items in this bowl. How many can you identify? Find: 1 violet, 1 faux fuchsia, 1 dipped corner wild rose, 1 rolled corner tea rose, 7 folded roses, 2 cabochon roses, 2 berries, 2 fantasy gathered flowers, 2 pansies, 2 prairie point leaves.

About the Author

Helen Gibb, a native of Australia now residing in the United States, has been designing in the craft industry for over 12 years. Her design work includes ribbon art, decorative painting, fabric painting, rubber stamping, silk florals, and children's kits. As a certified professional demonstrator in the craft industry, her skills are often tapped by manufacturers to test, develop, and demonstrate new products. She has taught a variety of classes, both nationally and internationally, written painting instruction books, and is the author of many projects featured in magazines such as *Crafts, Better Homes and Gardens, Needlework* and *Better Homes and Gardens Floral and Nature Crafts*.

Helen's awareness of ribbonwork began with the purchase of a bonnet from the late 1800s. Intrigued with millinery trimmings, her research led her to old millinery instruction books that not only described how to make hats, but how to trim them with bows and all types of ribbon floral effects.

Flowers and all things relating to them are prevalent in Helen's designs and she has consequently gained a reputation as the "flower lady." Her passion for ribbon flowers is evident when observing her exquisite floral creations found in the pages of this book.

Living in Colorado, Helen, her husband, and daughter enjoy the spectacular Rocky Mountains.

For more information about Helen's ribbon classes, workshops, and seminars, send a SASE to Springwood, 1002 Turnberry Circle, Louisville, CO 80027.

Bibliography

I have used a great many sources for my research into hats and ribbons. The following books have been most helpful and interesting. Some titles are no longer available but perhaps your local library could help you with a search for books that may still be in their systems.

Anlezark, Mildred. *Hats On Heads, The Art of Creative Millinery*. Kangaroo Press, Kenthurst, NSW, Australia, 1990

Art and Craft of Ribbon Work, The. Volumes 1 & 2, Antiquity Press, St. Helena, Calif.

Bawden, Juliet. *The Hat Book, Creating Hats for Every Occasion*. Lark Books, Asheville, N.C., 1993

Ben-Yusef, Anna. *Edwardian Hats*. R.L. Shep 1992, originally published 1909

Eckstein, Eve, and Firkins, June. *Hat Pins*. Shire Publications Ltd., Princes Risborough, Buckinghamshire, UK, 1992 and 1995

Gernsheim, Alison. *Victorian and Edwardian Fashion, A Photographic Survey*. Dover Publications, Inc., New York, 1963

Kaye, Georgina Kerr. *Millinery For Every Woman*. Lacis Publications, Berkeley, Calif., 1992, originally published 1926

Kingdom, Christine. *Glorious Ribbons*. Krause Publications, Iola, Wis., 1993

Lewis, Annabel. *The Ultimate Ribbon Book*. Trafalgar Square Publishing, Vt., 1995

Martin, Gene Allen. *Make Your Own Hats*. Houghton Mifflin Co., Boston, Mass., 1921

McDowell, Colin. *Hats. Status, Style and Glamour*. Rizzoli International Publications, Inc. New York, 1992

Montgomery Ward & Co. Catalogue and Buyers' Guide, 1895. Dover Publications, Inc., New York, 1969

Moore, Doris Langley. *The Woman in Fashion*. B.T. Batsford, Ltd., London, UK, 1949

National Cloak & Suit Co. *Women's Fashions of the Early 1900s*. 1909, Dover Publications, Inc., New York, 1992

Old Fashioned Ribbon Art. Dover Publications, Inc., New York, 1986

Pickens, Mary Brooks. *Old Fashioned Ribbon Trimmings and Flowers*. Dover Publications, Inc., New York, 1993, originally published 1922

Watkins, Susan. *Jane Austen In Style*. Thames and Hudson Publishers, London, 1996

Women's Institute of Domestic Arts and Sciences. *Ribbon Trimmings, A Course in Six Parts*. Dept. of Millinery. Sloane Publications, Martinez, Calif., 1992, originally published 1922

Ribbons, flowers, and feathers were all used to trim hats during the late 1800s. This group of hats is from the Edward B. Grossman & Company millinery and cloak catalog, 1898.

Resource Directory

There are many vendors who can supply you with all that is needed for ribbonwork. However, if you have difficulty in obtaining what you want, please contact these fine companies listed below.

Anne Brinkley Designs
12 Chestnut Hill Lane
Lincroft, NJ 07738
Phone (800) 633-0148
Fax (732) 530-3899
Wholesale. Framecraft porcelain and crystal boxes, needlework supplies.

Artemis
179 High St.
South Portland, ME 04106
Phone (207) 741-2509
Fax (207) 741-2497
Retail and wholesale. Bias cut, hand dyed silk ribbons by the yard or roll.

Berry Patch
300 Second Ave.
PO Box 893
Niwot, CO 80544
Phone & Fax (303) 652-1500
Retail. A huge selection of all ribbon types. Stamens, hats, millinery flowers, beads, crinoline, and books. Request a class schedule.

Frill Seekers
Shop 19 Westfield Shoppingtown
North Rocks, NSW 2151, Australia
Phone 02-9872-1951
Retail. Ribbons, needlework supplies, books, ribbon classes.

Hats by Leko
2081 Buffalo St.
Casper, WY 82604
Phone (307) 473-8881
Fax (307) 473-8883
Retail and wholesale. Blocked and unblocked straw and wool felt hats, berets, millinery supplies, books, patterns, ribbons, flowers, stamens, crinoline. Small charge for catalog.

Lacis
3163 Adeline St.
Berkeley, CA 94703
Phone (510) 843-7178
Fax (510) 843-5018
Retail and wholesale. Purse frames, stamens, crinoline, millinery supplies, books.

A Ladies Gallery
319 Main St.
Longmont, CO 80501
Phone (303) 702-0802
Retail. Lace and ladies fine period clothing and accessories, through early 1930s.

Lavender Fields
3542 Campfire Rd.
RORA D-9
Hartsel, CO 80449
Phone (719) 836-1519
Retail. Tea cozies, blouses, purses, and other bases for ribbonwork applications.

Loose Ends
3824 River Rd. N.
Salem, OR 97303
Phone (503) 390-7457
Fax (503) 390-4724
Retail and wholesale. Paper ivy "whips", papier mâché boxes.

Luzon Imports, Inc.
160 Southampton St.
Boston, MA 02118
Phone (800) 327-0008
Fax (617) 442-0226
Wholesale. Vine arbor, fairy love seat, nest bundle.

Mangelsen Enterprises
9706 Mockingbird Dr.
Omaha, NE 68127
Phone (402) 339-3922
Fax (402) 339-0208
Wholesale. Flower Fairies™, © The Estate of Cicely Mary Barker, 1997. Carved wooden mouse, arts, crafts, and decorative accessories.

CM Offray
Route 24, Box 601
Chester, NJ 07930
Phone (908) 879-4700
Wholesale. Ribbons.

Quilters' Resource Inc.
PO Box 148850
Chicago, IL 60614
Phone (800) 676-6543
Fax (773) 278-1348
Wholesale. Distributor of fine quilt and needle art supplies, beading threads, trims, books, and beautiful French wired and jacquard ribbons.

Ruban et Fleur
8655 S. Sepulveda Blvd.
Los Angeles, CA 90045
Phone (310) 641-3466
Fax (310) 641-1211
Retail and wholesale. Hats (blocked and unblocked), millinery trims, new and vintage ribbons, jacquards, passamentaries, stamens. Fabulous range of goodies.

S.A. Brown, Pty. Ltd.
52 Shepherd St.
Chippendale, NSW 2008, Australia
Phone 02-9319-7343
Retail and wholesale. Millinery supplies, ribbons, stamens, and books.

Vaban Gille, Inc.
165 Eighth St.
San Francisco, CA 94103
Phone (800) 448-9988
Fax (415) 255-2329
Wholesale. Beautiful French and Swiss wired ribbons. Vast selection of flower colors in addition to hundreds of styles of other ribbons. Papier mâché boxes.

The White Hyacinth
PO Box 266
Del Mar, CA 92014
Phone (619) 793-8384
Retail and wholesale. Designer cushions. Write for catalog.

YLI Corp.
161 West Main St.
Rock Hill, SC 29730
Phone (800) 296-8139
Silk embroidery ribbon, silk thread.

The Phipps Mansion is located at 3400 Belcaro Drive in Denver, Colorado 80209-4915 (phone 303-777-4441). Built between 1931 and 1933 at a cost of over $300,000, the Georgian style mansion was home to U.S. Senator Lawrence C. Phipps and his wife Margaret. It has 33,123 square feet of floor space and over 25 rooms. In addition to the fabulous design elements of the rooms, the mansion is a veritable treasure trove of furnishings, art, rare books, tapestries, antiques, and sculptures from around the world. The house is situated in a park-like setting of 5.5 acres. Bequeathed to the University of Denver in 1964, the mansion is now a venue for private receptions and corporate meetings. In 1997 it was host to a state dinner for the world's leaders attending the Summit of Eight Conference.

Index

A

Afternoon tea and tea cozy, 116
Autumn hat with mixed flowers, 109

B

Beaded fuchsias on a cream cushion, 118
Bears, 82
Berries, 35
Bluebells, 34
Bows, milliner's, 108
Boxes
      crystal vanity box, 86
      Victorian waxed roses on a box, 76
Brooches
      collage brooch with roses and fuchsias, 69
      wildwood brooch, 88

C

Calyx, 54
Cabochon rose lampshade, 80
Canterbury bells, 32
Carnations, 44
Classic rose cushion, 90
Collage brooch with roses and fuchsias, 69
Crinoline, 12
Chrysanthemum, 41
Cushions
      beaded fuchsias on a cream cushion, 118
      classic rose cushion, 90

D

Degas, 6
Delphiniums, 42

E

Edward B. Grossman, 9, 113, 122
Edward Ridley & Sons, 6, 103
Edwina in the arbor, 82

F

Fantasy flowers, 30
Filler flowers, 30
Floral tape, 13
Flower Fairy, 78, 84
Flowers
      berries, 35
      bluebells, 34
      Canterbury bells, 32

Flowers continued
      carnations, 44
      chrysanthemums, 41
      delphiniums, 42
      fantasy flowers, 30
      filler flowers, 30
      fuchsias, 38
            faux, 39
            frilly, 39
      gardenias, 48
      hollyhocks, 36
      multi-petal blossoms, 30
      pansies, 22
      peonies, 45
            fancy, 46
            quick, 45
      poppies, 28
      rose hips, 35
      roses, 55
            cabochon roses, 66
            cabochon rosebuds, 66
            folded roses, 59
            gathered roses, 57
            rosebuds, flat, 58
            tea roses, 62
                  basic, 62
                  blended, 64
            waxing, 77
            wild rose, 61
      sweet peas, 26
      violets, 24
Framed pansy bouquet, 74
Fuchsias, 38

G

Gardenias, 48

H

Hats, 102
      autumn hat with mixed flowers, 109
      spring hat with peony, 104
      vintage summer hat with roses, 106
      winter hat, 112
Hollyhocks, 36

L

Lampshade, 80
Leaves, 50

Leaves continued
    boat, 51
    mitered, 52
    prairie point, 50
        gathered, 50
        pleated, 51
    u-gathered, 51

M

Miniature rose bouquet for a crystal vanity box, 86
Multi-petal blossoms, 80

N

Nekclace, Victorian purse necklace, 93
Needles, 11

P

Pansies, 22
Peonies, 45
    fancy, 46
    quick, 45
Pins, long pins, 13
Poppies, 28
Purses
    vintage purse, 98
    wedding rose purse, 96

R

Ribbon
    cleaning, 11
    color and texture, 10
    quality, 10
    removing wire from, 15
    steaming, 15
    storage, 11
    types, 10
Ribbon flowers in garden urn, 72
Rose hips, 35
Roses, 55
    cabochon roses, 66
    cabochon rosebuds, 66
    folded roses, 59
    gathered roses, 57
    rosebuds, flat, 58
    tea roses, 62
        basic, 62
        blended, 64
    waxing, 77
    wild roses, 61

S

Scissors, 12

Spring hat with peony, 104
Stamens, 12
Stem wire, 13, 20
Stems, 20
    covered, 20
    ribbon, 54
    twisted ribbon, 54
    wire, 54
Stitches, 16
Sweet peas, 26

T

Techniques, 15
    folding, 16, 59
    gathering, 17
        on a wire, 17, 57
        straight stitch pattern, 17
        u-gather stitch pattern, 17, 57
    knots, 20
    petals, 18
        dipped corner, 18, 61
        rolled corner, 19, 62
    rolling, 16
    tubes, 20
    u-gather, 17
        continuous, 18, 64
        rolled edge, 18, 64
        single, 17, 64
Tea cozy, 116
Thread
    thread length, 11
    wrapping, 13
Tools, 11
Topiary of ivy and roses, 84

V

Velvet, distressing, 99
Victorian purse necklace, 93
Victorian waxed roses on a box, 76
Vintage purse, 98
Vintage summer hat with roses, 106
Violets, 24

W

Wedding rose purse, 96
Wildwood brooch, 88
Winter hat, 112
Woodland nest, 78

Other Books from Krause Publications

The Art and Craft of Paper Sculpture by Paul Jackson
The Banner Book by Ruth Ann Lowery
Beaded Adornment by Jeanette Shanigan
Beautiful Beads by Alexandra Kidd
Cash for Your Crafts by Wendy Rosen
Contemporary Decoupage by Linda Barker
Craft an Elegant Wedding by Naomi Baker and Tammy Young
The Crafter's Guide to Glues by Tammy Young
Crafting As a Business by Wendy Rosen
Creating & Crafting Dolls by Eloise Piper & Mary Dilligan
Creative Containers to Make and Decorate by Madeleine Brehaut
Creative Dollhouses From Kits by Robert Schleicher
Dazzle by Linda Fry Kenzie
The Design and Creation of Jewelry by Robert von Neumann
Dollmaking with Papier Mâché and Paperclay by Doris Rockwell Gottilly
Enamels, Enameling, Enamelists by Glenice Lesley Matthews
Exotic Beads by Sara Withers
Fabric Crafts & Other Fun with Kids by Susan Parker Beck and Charlou Lunsford
Fabulous Floorcloths by Caroline O'Neill Kuchinsky
Fanciful Frames by Juliet Bawden
Fantastic Finishes by Nancy Snellen
Fruits, Vegetables & Berries by Kally Ellis and Ercole Moroni
Gathering by Linda Fry-Kenzle
Glorious Greetings by Kate Twelvetrees
Glorious Ribbons by Christine Kingdom
How to Make Soft Jewelry by Jackie Dodson
How to Work in Stained Glass by Anita and Seymour Isenberg
Introduction to Lapidary by Pansy D. Kraus
The Irresistible Bead by Linda Fry Kenzle
Learn Bearmaking by Judi Maddigan
Modeling in Wax for Jewelry and Sculpture by Lawrence Kallenberg
Naturally Creative Candles by Letty Oates
New Ways With Polymer Clay by Kris Richards
The New Work of Our Hands by Mae Rockland Tupa
Painted Wooden Furniture by Cate Withacy
Paper Plus by Nancy Worrell
Papier Mâché Style by Alec MacCormick
Pigs, Piglets & Porkers by Alison Wormleighton
Quick and Easy Ways with Ribbon by Ceci Johnson
Sewing & Sculpting Dolls by Eloise Piper
Silk Flowers by Judith Blacklock
Silversmithing by Rupert Finegold and William Seitz
Snazaroo Zoo by Janis Bullis
StampCraft by Cari Haysom
Stamping Made Easy by Nancy Ward
Textile Artistry edited by Valerie Campbell-Harding
Three-Dimensional Decoupage by Letty Oates
Timeless Bouquets by Mireille Farjon
Treasures From the Earth by Kathy Lamancusa
Wedding Crafts by Lucinda Ganderton

Call 800-258-0929 to order